Book 4

Textbook in Mathematics for Class IV

MATH - MAGIC

राष्ट्रीय शैक्षिक अनुसंधान और प्रशिक्षण परिषद्
NATIONAL COUNCIL OF EDUCATIONAL RESEARCH AND TRAINING

First Edition
March 2007 Chaitra 1928

Reprinted
January 2008 Magha 1929
February 2009 Phalguna 1930
January 2010 Magha 1931
November 2010 Kartika 1932
January 2012 Magha 1933
December 2012 Arahayana 1934
December 2013 Arahayana 1935
December 2014 Arahayana 1936

PD 470T IJ

© *National Council of Educational Research and Training, 2007*

₹ 50.00

Printed on 80 GSM paper with NCERT watermark

Published at the Publication Division by the Secretary, National Council of Educational Research and Training, Sri Aurobindo Marg, New Delhi 110 016 and Printed at India Offset Printers (P.) Ltd., X-36, Okhla Industrial Area, Phase-II, New Delhi 110 020

ISBN 81-7450-698-5

OFFICES OF THE PUBLICATION DIVISION, NCERT

NCERT Campus
Sri Aurobindo Marg
New Delhi 110 016   Phone : 011-26562708

108, 100 Feet Road
Hosdakere Halli Extension
Banashankari III Stage
Bengaluru 560 085   Phone : 080-26725740

Navjivan Trust Building
P.O.Navjivan
Ahmedabad 380 014   Phone : 079-27541446

CWC Campus
Opp. Dhankal Bus Stop
Panihati
Kolkata 700 114   Phone : 033-25530454

CWC Complex
Maligaon
Guwahati 781 021   Phone : 0361-2674869

Publication Team

Head, Publication Division   : *N. K. Gupta*

Chief Production Officer   : *Kalyan Banerjee*

Chief Editor   : *Shveta Uppal*

Chief Business Manager   : *Gautam Ganguly*

Editor   : *Bijnan Sutar*

Production Assistant : *Sunil Kumar*

FOREWORD

The National Curriculum Framework (NCF), 2005, recommends that children's life at school must be linked to their life outside the school. This principle marks a departure from the legacy of bookish learning which continues to shape our system and causes a gap between the school, home and community. The syllabi and textbooks developed on the basis of NCF signify an attempt to implement this basic idea. They also attempt to discourage rote learning and the maintenance of sharp boundaries between different subject areas. We hope these measures will take us significantly further in the direction of a child-centred system of education outlined in the National Policy on Education (1986).

The success of this effort depends on the steps that school principals and teachers will take to encourage children to reflect on their own learning and to pursue imaginative activities and questions. We must recognise that given space, time and freedom, children generate new knowledge by engaging with the information passed on to them by adults. Treating the prescribed textbook as the sole basis of examination is one of the key reasons why other resources and sites of learning are ignored. Inculcating creativity and initiative is possible if we perceive and treat children as participants in learning, not as receivers of a fixed body of knowledge.

These aims imply considerable change in school routines and mode of functioning. Flexibility in the daily time-table is as necessary as rigour in implementing the annual calendar so that the required number of teaching days are actually devoted to teaching. The methods used for teaching and evaluation will also determine how effective this textbook proves for making children's life at school a happy experience, rather than a source of stress or boredom. Syllabus designers have tried to address the problem of curricular burden by restructuring and reorienting knowledge at different stages with greater consideration for child psychology and the time available for teaching. The textbook attempts to enhance this endeavour by giving higher priority and space to opportunities for contemplation and wondering, discussion in small groups, and activities requiring hands-on experience.

National Council of Educational Research and Training (NCERT) appreciates the hard work done by the Textbook Development Committee responsible for this book. We wish to thank the Chairperson of the Advisory Committee, Professor Anita Rampal and the Chief Advisor for this book, Professor Amitabha Mukherjee for guiding the work of this committee. Several teachers contributed to the development of this textbook; we are grateful to their principals for making this possible. We are indebted to the institutions and organisations which have generously permitted us to draw upon their resources, material and personnel. We are especially grateful to the members of the National Monitoring Committee, appointed by the Department of Secondary and Higher Education, Ministry of Human Resource Development under the Chairpersonship of Professor Mrinal Miri and Professor G.P. Deshpande, for their valuable time and contribution. As an organisation committed to the systemic reform and continuous improvement in the quality of its products, NCERT welcomes comments and suggestions which will enable us to undertake further revision and refinement.

New Delhi
20 November 2006

Director
National Council of Educational
Research and Training

TEXTBOOK DEVELOPMENT COMMITTEE

CHAIRPERSON, ADVISORY COMMITTEE FOR TEXTBOOKS AT THE PRIMARY LEVEL

Anita Rampal, *Professor*, Department of Education, Delhi University, Delhi

CHIEF ADVISOR

Amitabha Mukherjee, *Director*, Centre for Science Education and Communication (CSEC), Delhi University, Delhi

MEMBERS

Anita Rampal, *Professor*, Department of Education, Delhi University, Delhi

Asha Kala, *Primary Teacher*, MCD School, Krishi Vihar, G.K. Part I, New Delhi

Asmita Varma, *Primary Teacher*, Navyug School, Lodhi Road, New Delhi

Bhavna, *Lecturer*, DEE, Gargi College, New Delhi

Dharam Parkash, *Professor*, CIET, NCERT, New Delhi

Hema Batra, *Primary Teacher*, CRPF Public School, Rohini, Delhi

Jyoti Sethi, *Primary Teacher*, The Srijan School, Model Town, Delhi

Kanika Sharma, *Primary Teacher*, Kulachi Hansraj Model School, Ashok Vihar, Delhi

Prakasan V.K., *Lecturer*, DIET, Malappuram, Tirur, Kerala

Preeti Chadha Sadh, *Primary Teacher*, Basic School, CIE, Delhi University, Delhi

Suneeta Mishra, *Primary Teacher*, N.P. Primary School, Sarojini Nagar, New Delhi

MEMBER–COORDINATOR

Inder Kumar Bansal, *Professor*, DEE, NCERT, New Delhi

ILLUSTRATIONS AND DESIGN TEAM

Nancy Raj, Chennai

Anita Varma, Bangkok

S. Nivedita, Chennai

Srivi Kalyan, Harvard University

Sujasha Dasgupta, Gurgaon

Sougata Guha, The Srijan School, Model Town, Delhi

Arup Gupta, New Delhi

Cover Design: Sujasha Dasgupta

Layout and design support:

Anita Rampal, Sadiq Saeed and Sandeep Mishra

ACKNOWLEDGEMENTS

National Council of Educational Research and Training (NCERT) thanks the following persons and institutions for their contribution towards this textbook. Special thanks are due to the Centre for Science Education and Communication (CSEC), Delhi University, for providing academic support and hosting all the textbook development workshops. The teams were fully supported by the staff, who put in tremendous effort through long working hours even on holidays.

The Council gratefully acknowledges the contributions of Sandeep Mishra for the voluntary technical support and of Sadiq Saeed *(DTP Operator)*, Pratul Kumar Vasistha *(Copy Editor)*, Binod Kumar Jena *(Proof Reader)* and Shakamber Dutt *(Computer Station Incharge)* in shaping this book.

This book has drawn upon ideas from existing materials such as *Kunnimani* — Mathematics Textbooks for Class III & IV (developed by DPEP, Kerala for the Government of Kerala, 1997). The Council acknowledges the support of the *Chakmak* team at Eklavya, Bhopal for the children's drawings.

The Council also acknowledges the following teachers — P.K. Abdul Lathif and Cheggareddy F. C., Indira Ramesh, Sandhya Kumar — for participating in discussions and some book development workshops. The support offered by K.K. Vashishtha, *Head*, Department of Elementary Education, NCERT is also gratefully acknowledged.

The Council gratefully acknowledges the photographs taken by the following:

Chapter 1	—	*Anita Rampal, Gulab, Kabir Vajpeyi, Jugnu Ramaswamy, Y.K. Gupta, Seema K.K.* The contribution of *Vinyas Centre for Architectural Research & Design*, New Delhi and *Jagriti Public School*, Murshidabad, W.B. is also acknowledged.
Chapter 2	—	*Y.K. Gupta* (CIET, NCERT)
Chapter 3	—	*Mahesh Basedia, Sanchari Biswas, A.B. Saxena.* Thanks are also due to *Eklavya*, Bhopal.
Chapter 4	—	*Swati Gupta*
Chapter 5	—	*Suneeta Mishra, Y.K. Gupta* (CIET, NCERT)
Chapter 6	—	*Nitin Upadhye.* The Council also thanks the multimedia project 'Girl Stars', created by *Going to School* and supported by UNICEF, for the material on Kiran the 'Girl Star'.
Chapter 7	—	*Y.K. Gupta* (CIET, NCERT)
Chapter 12	—	*Sujasha Dasgupta, Y.K. Gupta* (CIET, NCERT)

MATH-MAGIC

What is inside this book?

Building with Bricks

Brick Patterns for Jagriti School

This is the true story of Jagriti School in Murshidabad (West Bengal). When its building was being made, there was a plan to make brick patterns on the floor and walls. Jamaal, Kaalu and Piyaar were the masons for the brick work. They wanted to get new ideas for the school building. So they took their other friends to see the old tomb of Murshid Kuli Khan. (See photos.)

This building has a big floor with about two thousand beautiful brick patterns. These were made by masons long back – about three hundred years ago.

Look how the bricks are arranged in these five floor patterns.

Which floor pattern do you like the most? _____

Have you seen such patterns anywhere?

The masons came back excited. Jamaal said — Ah! In those days they had made so many interesting brick patterns. We had forgotten these! Let us make some nice designs on the floor of this school.

Each mason made a different brick pattern. The school is proud to have such a beautiful building! Children play and sing on it and also make new patterns themselves.

❖ Which pattern is made in a circle?

❖ In which pattern can you show mirror halves? Draw a line.

❖ Now you draw some new floor patterns.

3

How to Draw a Brick?

These are two photos of the same brick.

In one photo we can see only one **face** of the brick. In the other we can see three faces. Circle the photo showing three faces.

❖ How many faces in all does a brick have? ____

❖ Is any face a **square**?

❖ Draw the smallest face of the brick.

❖ Which of these are the faces of a brick? Mark a (✓).

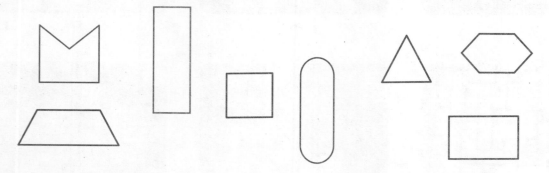

❖ Which of these is a drawing of a brick? Mark a (✓).

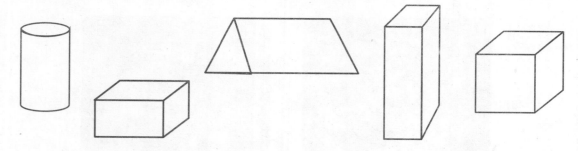

❖ Make a drawing of this box to show 3 of its faces.

❖ Can you make a drawing of a brick which shows 4 of its faces?

4

A Wall that will not Fall

One day Muniya and Zainab are playing with bricks and making their walls. Each makes a different wall.

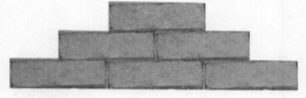
Zainab

Muniya

Zainab says her wall will not fall easily. Masons too do not put bricks one on top of the other, as Muniya has done.

What do you think? Which wall will be stronger?

Look for walls where you can see different brick patterns.

Different Wall Patterns

♣ Here are photos of three kinds of brick walls. Can you see the difference in the way the bricks are placed?

♣ Now match the photo of each wall with the correct drawing below:

Looking Through a Brick 'Jaali'

The masons who built Jagriti School had also made different *'jaali'* patterns on the walls.

❖ How many different *'jaali'* patterns can you see in these two photos?

This is a drawing of another beautiful *'jaali'*.

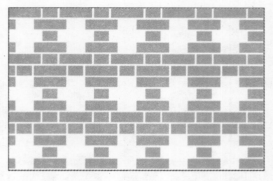

✤ Now colour some bricks red and make your own *'jaali'* patterns in the wall drawn below.

Can you see the window *(jharokha)* in this photo of the school?

✤ Now draw some *jharokha* patterns on the wall here. You can shade it black.

This *'jaali' is* from a library building in Kerala.

See how the edge of the bricks is used to make a **triangle** in the wall.

Have you seen bricks that look like triangles? Look at the bricks around the tree in this photo.

Do you see the **arch** in this photo?

This is from a school in Faizabad.

Find out

Look for other arches around you and draw them.

Have you seen arches in a bridge?

♣ Where else have you seen an arch?

_____

A Special Arch

In this photo from Orchha, see how the arch is made. It has a nice name – *Ghoonghat Waali Mehraab* (the arch with a veil).

Isn't the *'jaali'* of this window beautiful? It is made of thin bricks. Have you ever seen thin bricks? Look around.

Jamaal and Kaalu, the masons of Jagriti School, said that their grandfathers used many different kinds of bricks. Some of these are shown in this photo.

♣ Which of these bricks have curved edges?

♣ How many faces do you see of the longest brick?

♣ Is there any brick which has more than six faces?

Find Out: The Size of a Brick

Have you seen bricks of different sizes?

♣ Take one brick and measure it.

  a) How long is it? _____

  b) How wide is it? _____

  c) How high is it? _____

♣ Muniya wants to make a wall 1 metre long. How many bricks will she need to put in a line? _____

Bricks and Bricks — Hot and Fresh!

Ganesh and Sahiba live near a kiln where bricks are made.

♣ Can you guess how high is the chimney here? Is it:

  a) about 5 metres?

  b) about 15 metres?

  c) about 50 metres?

Ganesh and Sahiba love to look at the pattern of bricks in the long, long lines kept out to dry. They also watch how bricks are made.

Here are four pictures from the brick kiln. These pictures are jumbled up. Look at them carefully.

Write the correct order. _____

A

B

D

C

How do you think a brick is made out of soil dug from the earth? Look at the pictures and discuss in groups.

Have you seen a brick kiln? Did you try to guess the number of bricks kept there?

There are many, many brick kilns in India – thousands of them! More than **one hundred thousand**! Can you imagine how big this number is? This number is also called **one lakh**. Can you try to write it? Ask your friends where they have heard of a lakh.

Find out

Look at these photos and guess how many bricks are carried by this truck.

Also find out from a truck driver how many bricks they can carry in one truck.

Mental Math: Bhajan Buys Bricks

Bhajan went to buy bricks. The price was given for one thousand bricks. The prices were also different for different types of bricks.

Old bricks	— Rs 1200 for one thousand bricks
New bricks from Intapur	— Rs 1800 for one thousand bricks
New bricks from Brickabad	— Rs 2000 for one thousand bricks

Bhajan decided to buy the new bricks from Brickabad. He bought three thousand bricks. How much did he pay? _____

❖ Guess what he will pay if he buys 500 old bricks.

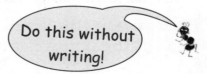

Do this without writing!

② Long and Short

How Far Apart are the Dots?

★ Guess the distance between any two dots. How many centimetres is it? Now measure it with the help of a scale. Did you guess right?

★ Which two dots do you think are farthest from each other? Check your answer.

★ Which two dots are nearest to each other? Check your answer.

Children can play this game in pairs, making dots on a plain sheet and asking their partner to guess the distance. This can also be extended to estimating bigger distances on the floor. The border of this chapter should also be used as a scale.

The Shorter Line

Akbar was a famous king. He had a smart minister called Birbal. Once Akbar gave him a difficult question. He drew a line on the floor.

Birbal, here is a line. Make it shorter without erasing.

Now your line is shorter.

———————————
Akbar's line

————————————————
Birbal's line

Look at the picture and explain how Birbal made Akbar's line shorter.

Now can you be as smart as Birbal? Make his line shorter without erasing it. Just think — is there any longest line?

Try This

★ Make her right arm 1 cm longer than the left arm.

★ Draw a cup 1 cm shorter than this cup.

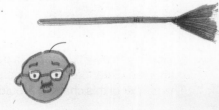

★ Draw a broom half as long as this broom.

★ Draw another hair of double the length.

14

How Tall Have You Grown?

Do you remember that in Class 3 you measured your height?

Do you think you have grown taller?

How much? _____ (cm)

Have your friends also grown taller?

Find out and fill the table below.

Friend's name	Last year's height (in cm)	This year's height (in cm)	How many cm have they grown?

Jhumpa once read a list of the tallest people in the world. One of them was 272 cm tall! That is just double of Jhumpa's height. How tall is Jhumpa? _____ cm.

> Wow! His height is exactly double my height.

Imagine

★ Could that person pass through the door of your classroom without bending?

★ Will his head touch the roof of your house if he stands straight?

The Long and Short of Your Family!

★ Who is the tallest in your family? _____

★ Who is the shortest in your family? _____

★ What is the difference between their heights? _____

15

Inter-School Sports Meet

Race

This is a 100 metre race for girls. Arundhati is nearest the finishing line. She is about 6 metres from it.

Behind her is Rehana. Konkana and Uma are running behind Rehana. Look at the picture. To answer the questions below choose from these distances:

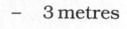

- 3 metres

- 6 metres

- 10 metres

- 15 metres

Rehana

6 metres

a) How far is Rehana from Arundhati? _____

b) How far ahead is Rehana from Konkana and Uma? _____

c) How far are Konkana and Uma from the finishing line? _____

Have you heard about a 1500 m or 3000 m race? (You remember that 1000 metres make 1 kilometre and 500 metres make half a kilometre.)

★ So you can say —

In a 1500 metres race people run _____ km

In a 3000 metres race people run _____ km

Have you heard about marathon races in which people have to run about 40 kilometres? People run marathons on roads

Here are the Indian Records and World Records for some jumps.

Find out from the table —

1. How many centimetres more should Chandra Pal jump to equal the Men's World Record for high jump?

2. How many centimetres higher should Bobby A. jump to reach 2 metres?

   Remember that 1m = 100 cm

   Half metre = ?

3. Galina's long jump is nearly

17

a)   7 metres

Sports	World Record	Indian Record
High Jump (Men)	Javier S. (2m 45 cm)	Chandra Pal (2m 17 cm)
Long Jump (Men)	Mike P. (8m 95 cm)	Amrit Pal (8m 8 cm)
High Jump (Women)	Stefka K. (2m 9 cm)	Bobby A. (1m 91 cm)
Long Jump (Women)	Galina C. (7m 52 cm)	Anju G. (6m 83 cm)

b)   7 and a half metres

c)   8 metres

4. Look at the Women's World Records. What is the difference between the longest jump and the highest jump?

5. If Mike P. could jump _____ centimetres longer, his jump would be full 9 metres.

6. Whose high jump is very close to two and half metres?

   a)   Stefka K.

   b)   Chandra Pal

   c)   Javier S.

   d)   Bobby A.

Running Exercise

The doctor has told Devi Prasad to run 2 km every day to stay fit. He took one round of this field. How far did he run?

The field was very far from his home. So he chose a park nearby. The boundary of the park was about 400 metres long.

★ How many rounds of the park must Devi Prasad run to complete 2 km?

★ One day the weather was very good and a cool breeze was blowing. He felt so good that he kept jogging till he got tired after 8 rounds. That day he ran _____ km and _____ metres !

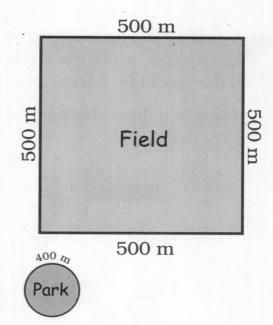

How Many Rooms High?

The Qutab Minar is 72 metres high.

About how many metres high is your classroom?

Guess how many rooms, one on

top of the other, will be equal to the Qutab Minar. _____

Explain how you made a guess.

From Kozhikode to Thalassery

Subodh is going to Kozhikode which is 24 kilometres (km) away. Manjani is going to Thalassery which is 46 km away in the opposite direction.

How far is Kozhikode from Thalassery? _____

How Far is Your Home from School?

Momun comes to school from very far. He first walks about

400 metres to the pond. With slippers in his hands, he then walks 150 metres through the pond. Next he runs across the 350 metres wide green field. Then he carefully crosses the 40 metres wide road to reach his school.

How much does Momun walk every day to reach school? _____

Is it more than 1 km? _____

★ Find out how far your friends live from school and fill the table. Write in metres or kilometres.

Who among you lives nearest to the school? _____

Who lives farthest from the school? _____

How many children live less than 1 kilometre away from your school? _____

Is there anyone who lives more than 5 km away from the school? How do they come to school? _____

Friend's name	Distance of home from school

_____

Guess and Find Out

1. How long is the thread in a reel?

2. How long is the string of a kite reel? Can it be more than a kilometre long?

3. If a handkerchief is made out of a single thread, how long would that thread be?

I Wish I Were

Try to find out:

1. Which is the highest building that you have seen? About how many rooms high was it?

2. How high can a kite go? Can it go higher than the Qutab Minar?

Children will get a good idea of 1 kilometre distance if it is possible to take them for a 1 km walk, preferably along a straight path.

3. How high can a plane fly? Can it fly higher than Mount Everest

I wish I were a kite
So that I could rise
Above this building's height.

I wish I were a bird
So that I could fly
And reach above that kite.

I wish I were a cloud
So that I could move
Above those little birds.

I wish I were a plane
So that I could rise
Above the clouds and the hills.

which is about 9 km high?

4. Have you ever seen clouds below you?

It would be useful here to discuss about children's experiences, particularly when talking about clouds and their height, so that they get an intuitive feel of relative heights, and can begin to estimate large distances.

③ A Trip to Bhopal

Today Sugandha is very excited. All the children of her school are going on a trip to Bhopal with their teachers. Ms. Meenakshi and Mr. Rakesh are talking about the number of buses needed.

Ms. Meenakshi — We will need 4 buses.

Mr. Rakesh — I think we need at least 5.

Ms. Meenakshi — Each bus has 50 seats.

Mr. Rakesh — Let us see how many children are going.

Class	Number of children
I	33
II	32
III	42
IV	50
V	53
Total	_____

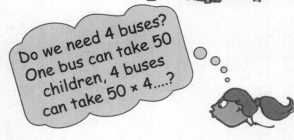

Do we need 4 buses? One bus can take 50 children, 4 buses can take 50 × 4....?

✤ So there are a total of _____ children going.

✤ If they get 4 buses, how many children will get seats? _____

✤ Will there be any children left without seats?

For just a few children, we can't get another bus!

We can share seats.

Children should be encouraged to estimate first and then find out the answer using any method they want. It is important to discuss the methods children use to solve a problem.

Waiting for the Buses

Sahiba jumps out of the line to see if the buses are coming. She shouts loudly — Hey! I can see them. Run! Grab the window seats.

Many children start jumping in excitement. But ....

Stop! What is this? These buses are so small!

Now there is an argument.

We told you to bring big buses!

We did not have enough big buses. So we got many mini buses.

Each mini bus can take 35 students. How many mini buses are needed?

_____

Come on now, get in fast. It's already 9 o'clock.

The Journey Begins

As the buses start moving, children sing at the top of their voices. Some look outside to enjoy the view of the green fields and the hills.

Indra — When will we reach Bhopal?

Ms. Asha — If we don't stop anywhere, we should reach there in 2 hours, that is around _____ o' clock.

Manjeet   — Is it very far?

Mr. Bhimsen   — It is about 70 km.

Ruby   — Are we going to stop anywhere?

Mr. Rakesh   — May be at Bhimbetka, about 50 km from here.

♣ If they go to Bhimbetka, they will reach there

— Before 10 o'clock

— Between 10 o'clock and 11 o' clock

— After 11 o' clock

As they are talking, Bahadur shouts — Hey! look at the Narmada. Everyone looks out of the windows.

Ruby — Wow! it is soooo long and so wide!
             Let us guess how wide it is.

Gopi — Uhm---m, 100 metres? No, it is much more. Can't say.

Victoria — It must be more than half a kilometre.

Ms. Asha — Look, it is written – 'This bridge is 756.82 metres long'. So we can guess that the Narmada must be about 500 metres wide at this place.

♣ Was Victoria right ?

Sadaf — I just can't imagine 500 metres.

Ms. Asha — See, our bus is about 5 metres long. Imagine how many buses can stand in a line on this bridge.

♣ Have you ever crossed a long bridge? About how many metres long was it? _____

Everyone looks down at the river.

Mr. Rakesh — The water level now is quite low. It must be about 40 metres below the bridge.

Ms. Asha — But in the rainy season, the water had risen. Then it was just about 15 metres below the bridge.

♣ What is the difference between the water level of the Narmada in the rainy season and now? _____ metres.

The children discuss about the river for some time. ......

Suddenly, the bus stops with a jerk.

Oh! The petrol pump. Two buses need to be refilled.

The buses stand in a line. Children are sticking their necks out to see how diesel is filled in the bus. Some children have got down to look more closely.

✤ Each bus takes about 15 minutes to refill and there are two buses to be refilled. So they stop there for about _____ minutes, which means they are late by about _____ minutes.

Ltrs 100.00
RS 3500.00
Diesel

Rupees: 175.00
Litres: 5
Rate per Litre: 35.00

Hey it has such a big tummy! It has already taken 100 litres.

So we have to pay 3500 Rupees for the diesel!

✤ Look in the picture and find the price of 1 litre of diesel. _____

As the buses are being refilled, some children go to the toilet near the petrol pump.

How much time did Aman take to come out of the toilet? _____

Aman has taken as much time to empty himself as one bus is taking to refill!

To Bhimbetka

After the buses are refilled, the journey starts again. Now the children are told that they are stopping at Bhimbetka.

Anjan — What is Bhimbetka?

Ms. Raina — It's a place with lots of caves and cave-paintings made by people ten thousand years ago.

Sumonto — Ten tho....uu....saa....nd years! I cannot even think of one thousand years back!

Gopi — Oh! one thousand years is a big thing, I can't even think of one hundred years.

Gauri — I can think of 100 years because my father's grandmother is 100 years old.

Manjeet — That means those caves are almost hundred great grandmothers old!!

Everybody bursts into laughter – Ha! Ha! Ha!

Now the children are really excited to see the cave-paintings. It is about 11 o' clock when they reach Bhimbetka.

28

Shankar — This painting also has very big bisons. Hey, I got an idea. I will count the bisons and you count the deer in the paintings.

Bonomala — I will count people. Let us see which are the most — bisons, deer or people.

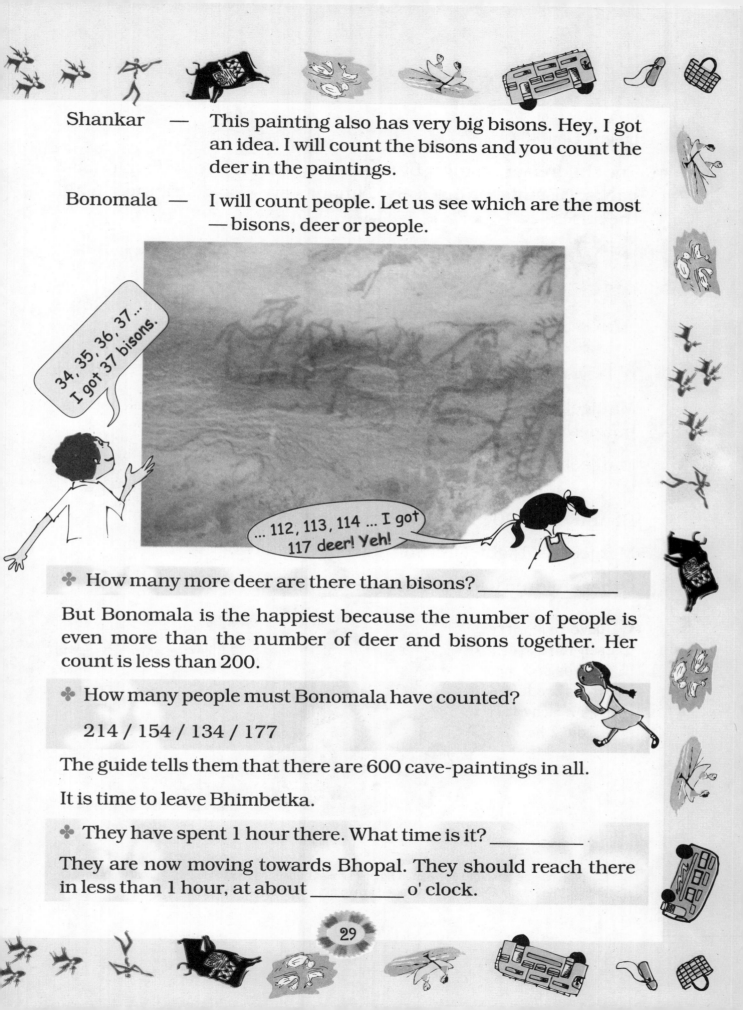

34, 35, 36, 37 ... I got 37 bisons.

... 112, 113, 114 ... I got 117 deer! Yeh!

♣ How many more deer are there than bisons? _____

But Bonomala is the happiest because the number of people is even more than the number of deer and bisons together. Her count is less than 200.

♣ How many people must Bonomala have counted?

214 / 154 / 134 / 177

The guide tells them that there are 600 cave-paintings in all.

It is time to leave Bhimbetka.

♣ They have spent 1 hour there. What time is it? _____

They are now moving towards Bhopal. They should reach there in less than 1 hour, at about _____ o' clock.

Lunch Time

The children are hungry by this time so they take out their lunch-packs. Biscuits, oranges and bananas are also distributed in all the buses.

Each child is to be given 1 orange, 1 banana and 5 biscuits.

All the children take oranges and biscuits but 38 children do not take bananas.

♣ How many oranges, biscuits and bananas are distributed?

Manjeet and Bhanu quickly finish their lunch and start asking puzzles to pass the time.

Manjeet — Tell me the number which is exactly between 100 and 150.

Bhanu — 120 … no, 130 … no it is 125.

Manjeet — Right. OK! You ask now.

Other children join in. Everyone is asking puzzling questions.

A I gave four toffees each to four of my friends and three toffees are left with me. How many toffees did I have?

B What numbers can you make using 3, 5 and 7? You can make 357 and 537. What others?

C A number becomes double if it is increased by 8. What is the number?

Children can be asked to solve many more similar questions or puzzles, both orally and in writing. They should also be encouraged to explain the strategies they use.

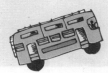

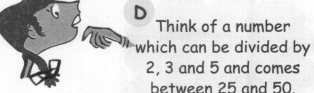

D Think of a number which can be divided by 2, 3 and 5 and comes between 25 and 50.

E A small ant climbs 3 cm in 1 minute but slips down 2 cm. How much time will it take to climb to 2 cm?

Can you solve these? Try them out.

Which Boat do We Take?

They are so lost in puzzles that they do not notice they have reached the lake. It is a very big lake with a small island in it.

The lake looks very beautiful at this time. There are a lot of ducks making a loud noise. Some children give them popcorn.

Now comes the exciting part! It is time to go for boating. They have to choose which boat to take. But that is not easy.

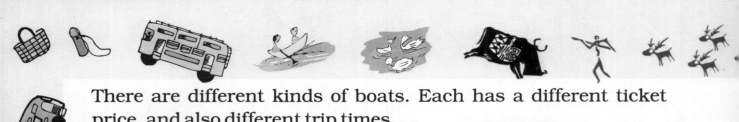

There are different kinds of boats. Each has a different ticket price, and also different trip times.

Name of the Boat	Ticket-price	Trip-time
1. Double-decker	Rs 30	45 minutes
2. Paddle-boat	Rs 15	30 minutes
3. Motor-boat	Rs 25	20 minutes
4. Boat with oars	Rs 15	45 minutes

Four of us will take a paddle boat and race with Gauri and her group.

We will take the motor-boat. It is costly but fun — Zooo...m!

Based on the table showing ticket rates, trip time etc. some questions are given in the book. Children should be motivated to make many more questions themselves.

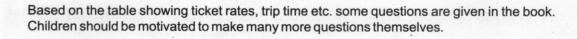

32

> Let us take the oar-boat. It is not costly and we get more time for a peaceful ride.

> Hey! We are going on the double-decker. It also has music. It costs a lot but we get more time.

♣ Indra and Bhanu first went in the motor-boat, and then took the oar-boat.

How much did they pay for both the boats? Rs _____

How much time did they get for both rides? _____

♣ One group of children went for the double-decker trip. They paid Rs 450 in total. How many children went for the double-decker trip? _____

♣ Which boat makes two trips in 1 hour?

♣ Which boat takes less than half an hour to complete a trip?

♣ Which boat gives them the most time taking the least money?

♣ Javed went twice for boating. He paid a total of Rs 40. and boated for 50 minutes. Which two boats did he take? _____

Time to Return

Children enjoy different boat rides till 4 o'clock. It is time to return. Now they will not stop anywhere and reach back in two hours.

So, they should reach Hoshangabad by _____ o'clock.

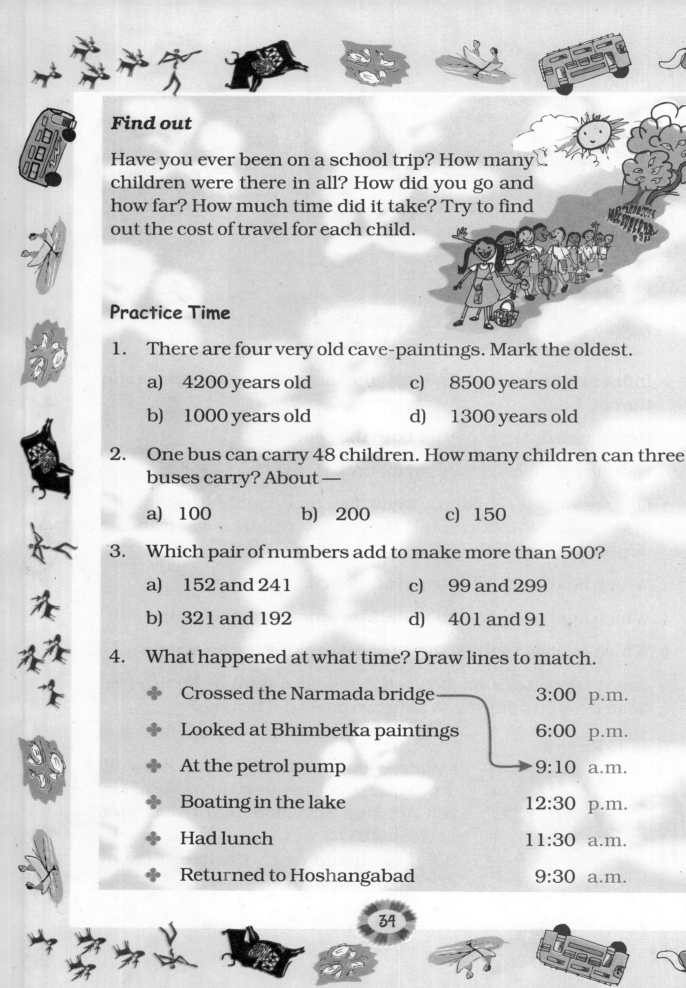

Find out

Have you ever been on a school trip? How many children were there in all? How did you go and how far? How much time did it take? Try to find out the cost of travel for each child.

Practice Time

1. There are four very old cave-paintings. Mark the oldest.

   a) 4200 years old

   b) 1000 years old

   c) 8500 years old

   d) 1300 years old

2. One bus can carry 48 children. How many children can three buses carry? About —

   a) 100   b) 200   c) 150

3. Which pair of numbers add to make more than 500?

   a) 152 and 241

   b) 321 and 192

   c) 99 and 299

   d) 401 and 91

4. What happened at what time? Draw lines to match.

   ♣ Crossed the Narmada bridge   3:00 p.m.

   ♣ Looked at Bhimbetka paintings   6:00 p.m.

   ♣ At the petrol pump   9:10 a.m.

   ♣ Boating in the lake   12:30 p.m.

   ♣ Had lunch   11:30 a.m.

   ♣ Returned to Hoshangabad   9:30 a.m.

34

Practice Time

1) Three friends read time from a clock. Who is right?

	Cheeku	Bittu	Pinki
	12:03	12:15	3:00
	7:25	5:07	5:35
	3:35	7:03	7:15

2) **Show the following times in the clock:**

3:10

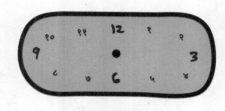

6:40

4:45

2:20

3:15

7:35

Do you like sky watching? If yes, then this one should interest you:

a) At what time does the sun rise at your place? ———

b) When does the sun set? ———

Dose the sun rise and set at the same times every day?

Look at a newspaper and see the time of sunrise and sunset in different months.

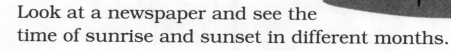

Look at the photo and guess the time at this place.

This photo was taken in Paris, France. In Paris the sun sets after 9 pm at night during summer. This photo was taken at night! But in winter it becomes dark here by 4 pm in the evening.

3) **Find out**

✳ How long will it take the minute hand to move from

a) to _____ c) to _____

b) to _____ d) to _____

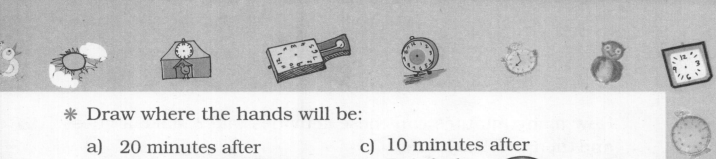

* Draw where the hands will be:

a) 20 minutes after 6 o' clock

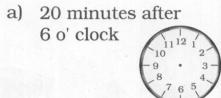

c) 10 minutes after 7 o' clock

b) 30 minutes after 8 o' clock

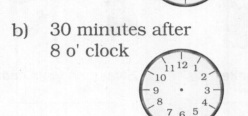

d) 15 minutes after 5 o' clock

* How long does your school assembly take? _____

How long is your lunch break? _____

How long is your games period? _____

Is it the same as all the other periods? _____

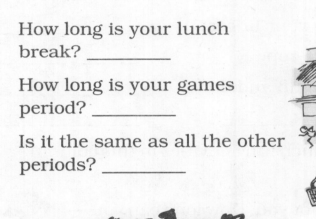

The games period and lunch break seem very short! Aren't they?

* How many minutes can these activities take? Make a guess and then check at home.

Boiling 1 litre milk
_____

Filling a bucket
_____

Sweeping your room
_____

Activity Time

* In one minute, how many times can you —

a) Snap your finger   _____

b) Skip a rope   _____

c) Jump up and down   _____

d) _____   _____

Write more such fun activities in this column.

* Here is another challenge for you. How long can you —

a) Speak non-stop _____

b) Stand on one leg _____

c) Sing 'Aaaaa….' without a break _____

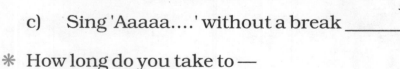

* How long do you take to —

a) Run a 50 metre race _____

b) Collect 50 pebbles from the ground _____

c) Count 1 to 100 _____

Who is the winner?

✳ Let's look at a clock again! Solve this one —

a) The minute hand started from '2'. How many minutes will it take to come back to '2' again? _____

b) What happens to the hour hand? Does it also move? How long will it take to move from one number to the next?

c) Look around you and list the activities that take about one hour to complete.

1. _____

2. _____

3. _____

4. _____

5. _____

How long does it take to cook dinner at home?

More than an hour/less than an hour.

Ask your father if he can cook as fast as your mother does.   Yes / No

Which games take less than an hour to finish? _____

How long does a football match take?

Children will enjoy doing activities to see all the things they can do in one minute. Observing activities at home will give them a sense of time and also help them value the effort of others.

Rani's Diary

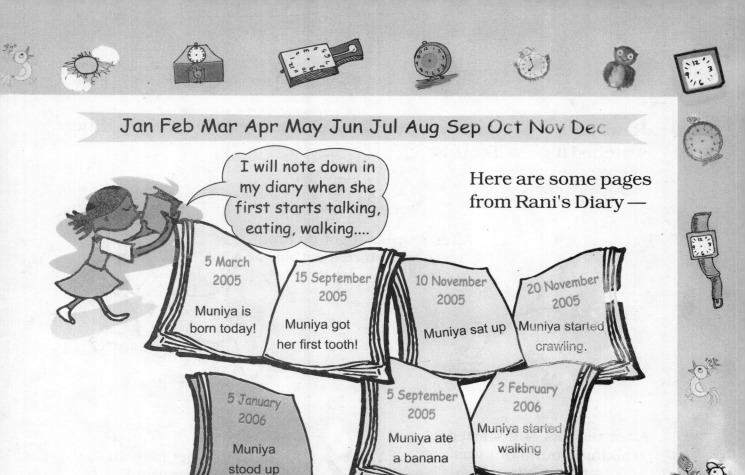

Here are some pages from Rani's Diary —

Mark these in the correct order on Muniya's Time Line.

5/3/05

Was born

* Muniya got her first tooth in September. How many months old was she then? How many months have passed from March to September? _____

* How old was Muniya, when

(a) she first sat up? _____

(b) she got her first tooth? _____

* What did she do first — 1) walking/eating a banana?

2) crawling/standing?

43

Rani had a pet puppy. After 2 weeks it opened its eyes. She watched it grow like this:

After 3 weeks it got its first teeth and started eating.

After 4 weeks — it started walking around but was still wobbling.

It had a full set of teeth by the time it was 7 months old.

After 1 year, it was a grown-up dog and got its own puppies.

✳ Now make a time-line of this dog's life in your notebook.

✳ Note the differences between Muniya and Rani's puppy:

Positions	Muniya (age)	Puppy (age)
Started walking		
Ate food for the first time		
Got the first tooth		

44

Find out

Do all animals grow at the same speed?

Discuss about the growth of —

1. A hen
2. A cow
3. A bird

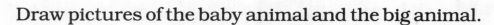

Draw pictures of the baby animal and the big animal.

Here are the pictures of grandfathers posing for a photograph. Who looks the oldest to you?

Elephant Appu's
grandfather
(95 years old)

Chuchoo rat's
grandfather
(2 years old)

Rani's
grandfather
(70 years old)

* How much older is Appu's grandfather than Rani's grandfather? _____

* Will Chuchoo's grandfather ever grow as old as Appu's grandfather? _____

* How much younger is Chuchoo rat's grandfather than Rani's grandfather? _____

This is a good opportunity for children and teachers to find out about the life spans and growth patterns of different animals. The idea is to compare and discuss without having to memorise any such information.

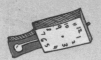

Holidays are Fun!

Atif's holidays had begun. He was very excited. He had made some wonderful plans and wanted to tell his cousin Shabana. So he wrote her a letter —

Ajmer
1/5/06

Dear Shabana aapa,

Hello!

How are you? I am fine here. Aapa, my holidays have started from today! I am going to my Nani's place on 5/5/06. I will be back on 20/5/06. My school will reopen on 30/6/06. When does your school close? Why don't you come here? We will have great fun!

Bye for now

Atif

Shabana who stays in Nagpur, got this letter on 6/5/06. She wrote back to Atif —

Nagpur
7/5/06

Dear Atif,

Hello!

I am doing well here. I got your letter yesterday. Happy holidays! My school will close on 1st June 2006. It will reopen on 10th August. I will go on a school trip to Goa and will return on 7/6/06. I will try to come to Ajmer after that. Bye

Shabana

Atif wrote his letter on 1/5/06. You remember how we write a date in numbers?

1/5/06 is 1 May 2006.

46

Now write which dates these stand for –

5/5/06   5 May 2006 _____

20/5/06   _____

7/6/06   _____

1/1/07   _____

Write these dates in numbers.

1 June 2006 _____

30 May 2006 _____

10 Aug 2007 _____

* How long did it take the letter to reach from Ajmer to Nagpur?_____

* How many days will Atif spend at his Nani's place? _____

* Fill in the table:

	Dates		Number of days
	From	To	
Shabana's holidays			
Atif's holidays			

Who has got longer holidays — Shabana or Atif?

* Which long holidays do you get in school? Fill the table.

Occassion	Dates		Number of days
	From	To	
Summer holidays			
Autumn Break			
Winter Break			
Holidays after the exam			

On 15 May 2006 Chandran went to a shop to buy butter. He checked the packet to see if this butter was safe to eat.

It was written on the packet — Best before 180 days from the date of packing.

Then he checked the date of packing. It was 15/01/06.

Help him find out if he should buy this butter or not.

— In which month was the butter packed? _____
— Which month will it be 180 days after 15/01/06? _____
— Can Chandran eat it on 15th May 2006? _____

Do you ever check the date of packing of things you buy?

Have you seen medicines which have the **expiry date** written on them? It tells you after which date it is unsafe to take the medicine.

Find Out

* Which are the other things that come with an expiry date?

On a cough syrup it was written:

Mfg. date   07/03

This shows it was made in July 2003.

Exp. date   07/05

This shows the month and year till when it is safe to take.

* What month and year is written as 07/05? _____

Would it be safe to take the cough syrup in September 2005? _____

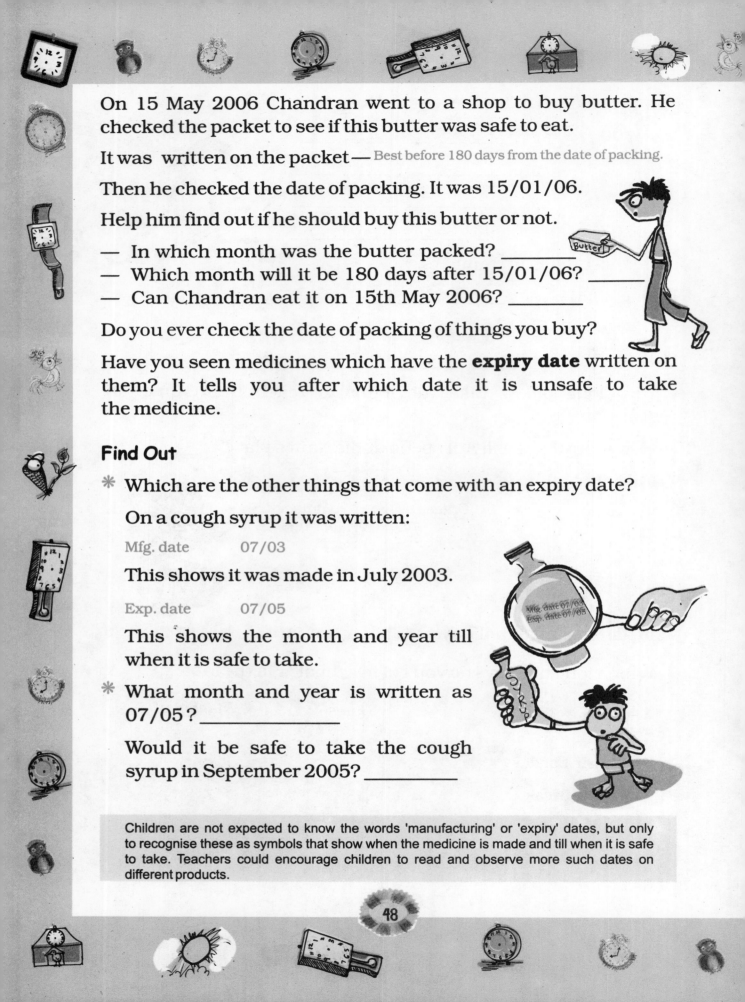

Children are not expected to know the words 'manufacturing' or 'expiry' dates, but only to recognise these as symbols that show when the medicine is made and till when it is safe to take. Teachers could encourage children to read and observe more such dates on different products.

Tutun Missed the Train

Tutun's school had closed for the summer holidays. He went to his grandma's place. He met a lot of his cousins there. He was enjoying himself and didn't want to go back home.

Tutun, pack your bag. The train leaves at 5:30 in the evening.

Oh no! We are going back so soon! I wish we miss our train

Tutun and his parents reached the station at 5:15. But guess what? They had actually missed the train!

Hurray! That means I am not going back today.

Can you guess why they missed the train?

Actually the train had left at 5:30 in the morning! Tutun's parents were upset. They asked the station master —

Our ticket says 5:30.

But Sir, this means 5:30 in the morning.

Oh yes. How could I forget that?

The Railways will write 17:30 for 5:30 in the evening.

Why??

Because they use a 24-hour clock.

Look at this chart. It tells the difference between your watch and a 24-hour clock. Try to complete it.

Time by your watch (12-hour clock)	Time by a 24-hour clock
1 o' clock in the afternoon	13:00 hours
2 o' clock in the afternoon	14:00 hours
3 o' clock in the afternoon	_____
3:30 in the afternoon	15:30 hours
6 o' clock in the evening	_____
9 o' clock in the evening	_____
12 o' clock at midnight	_____

Now can you tell why a 24-hour clock is called so?

Suppose a train leaves at 8:30 at night. The time written on the Railway ticket would be _____.

In a 12-hour clock, each time comes twice in a day.
So 5:30 in the morning is 5:30 am.
   5:30 in the evening is 5:30 pm.

What about 12:30 in the afternoon?

That is 12:30 pm. After 12 o'clock at noon we use pm till midnight.

You must have noted the time of sunrise and sunset.

Write here using am and pm.

Time of Sunrise	
Time of Sunset	

Where have you seen a 24-hour clock being used?

1. _____

2. _____

3. _____

⑤ The Way The World Looks

Gappu's Air Journey

Gappu was a brave little mouse. One day, he saw children playing with a huge gas balloon. The balloon went up and touched the roof. Gappu was thrilled. He got an idea. Next day, when the children went to school, Gappu climbed up the string of the balloon. He could see the blades of the fan from above.

Oh! There is so much dirt on these blades. From below they look so clean.

✤ Draw how the fan looks from below.

Gappu looked down. He could see the bed, the chair, one table with books on it and the other table with a bottle, a jug, fruits etc.

✤ Look for these things in the photo.

That stupid Chinky is looking for cheese. Can't even see it is kept on top of the jug.

The story demands a high level of imagination and children need adequate discussion about how things look differently in shape and size when you see them from different views and distances. However, the story should not lose its fun element.

✤ Can you think why Gappu could see the cheese on the jug but Chinky could not?

Just then a strong wind pushed the balloon out of the room.

> When I ran around in my house, it looked so big! But from here, it looks small. How is that?

The balloon flew up and Gappu started going up in the sky. As he looked down, he could see his house.

As he went higher he could see things around his house — the park, the Gurudwara, the railway-line, a sweet-shop and Suhasini's house with the big water-tank on its roof …

> Who is that, on the railway track? Is it that fat cat Monty? Ha! Ha! Ha! From here it looks like a big white mouse.

> This must be the Gurudwara where Amarjeet goes every day.

> I did not know there is a sweet shop here! Yummy!

❖ Imagine how your classroom looks from above. Try to draw it and mark the benches, blackboard, doors, windows etc.

The balloon went up, up and up. Gappu kept wondering how big the world is! Now he could see lots of houses, streets, roads and buses.

Suddenly, there was a loud sound ... *phatt*! The balloon burst and started falling down ... down ... and everything started looking bigger and bigger. *Dhapp*! --- Gappu fell on the railway-track. He ran to save himself from the cruel Monty who ran after Gappu and the other rats on the railway track.

When Gappu saw the railway-track from above, it looked like this —

But when he fell on the track, the railway line looked like this.

Oh! Things look so different when you look at them from the top and from the side.

♣ Look at these pictures and discuss why things look wide and big at this end but narrow and small at the other end.

Match Two Views of the Same Pose

This is a top view of a girl in a yoga pose.

Only one of the photos below is the correct match of the same yoga pose. Mark it.

These are two different views of the same bowls.

✤ In which photo are the bowls upside down? _____

Look at the side view in photo 3 to find the answer.

✤ Draw lines to match the side view with the top view of

— A pipe

— A funnel

✤ Try to draw pictures of a shoe from the side, top, front etc.

It would be exciting for children to imagine and find out how different things can look from different angles. It also helps to improve their spatial understanding.

The Park behind Gappu's House

Do you remember the park behind Gappu's house?

Here is a bigger picture of that park. Look at it carefully and answer the questions.

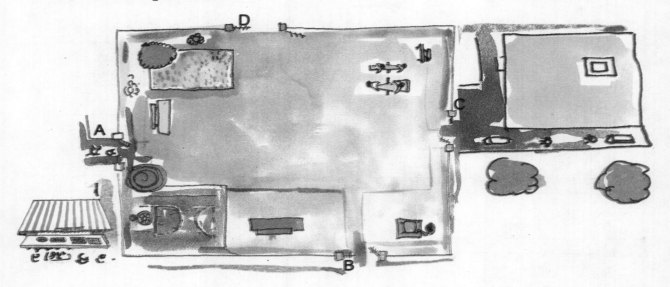

✤ Mark the gate nearest to the sweet shop. A / B / C / D

✤ Which gate is nearest to Gappu's house?

✤ If you enter from gate B, the green bench will be to your —

Left / Right / Front

✤ When Suhasini entered the park, the flower bed was to her right. Which gate did she enter from?

✤ Which of these is nearest to you if you enter from gate C?

1. Basketball court   2. Flower bed

3. Green bench   4. See-saw

Young children tend to think of directions like left, front etc. in absolute terms. It is important for the development of spatial understanding to make them aware that directions are relative to one's position. Something that is towards the left from one position can be towards the right from another position. More activities can be done in the class based on this concept.

Ismail's Home

On the phone Ismail told Srijata the route to his house from her house. The route map is shown here.

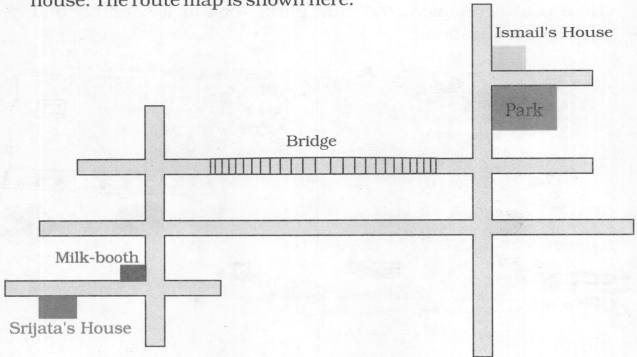

This is what Ismail told Srijata:

 "From your house, reach the milk-booth and then take a left turn. From the second crossing take a right turn and go over the bridge. Go straight and then take the first right turn. After about 100 metres you will see a big park.

When you cross the park you will come to a side lane. My house is the first house in that lane.

❖ Did Ismail go wrong somewhere? Can you correct him?

❖ Show where Srijata will reach if she takes the route he told her.

❖ Write the directions for going from Ismail's house to Srijata's house.

Gibli and the Big Box

Do you remember Gibli the ant in the Math-Magic Book 3?

Well, one day Gibli saw a big box on her way. It looked like this.

Gibli moved across and turned left. Now she could see the other face of the big box.

Gibli was confused. What was this box? She climbed on a cup and tried to see from there. The box looked like this.

Can you guess what that box-like thing was?

The numbers on the opposite faces of this box add up to 7.

* Which number was on the opposite side of 5?

* In the picture, which number will be at the bottom?

* Which number will Gibli see if she again turns left from 5?

* What will this box look like if you opened it up? Mark the correct picture.

A

```
  3
2 1 5
  4
  6
```

B

```
  3
6 1 5
  4
  2
```

C

```
  4
2 1 6
  5
  3
```

D

```
  3
2 1 5
  6
  4
```

Try it out

Draw a shape like this on a thick paper. Cut it out and colour the different faces in different colours.

Can you use this box to play a game?

6 The Junk Seller

Have you ever met a *Kabariwali* – a woman who sells junk? This is a true story told by Kiran, who has a junk shop in Patna.

 I studied in a Hindi medium school in my village. My father wanted girls to study like boys. I loved Hindi and Science, but I hated Maths! Today Maths is most useful for my work. I could never imagine this in school.

What about you? Do you also find Maths difficult?

What is the most difficult thing in your Maths book?_____

What do you think is the easiest lesson? _____

When I was young, my father died in an accident. So my mother worked as a servant in some houses. We had a difficult time. I had to leave school after Class VIII. I wanted to study more but my mother got me married.

My husband's family lived in a mud house. His two brothers and his sister did not go to school. He had a tea stall.

Find out: how much for a cup of tea?

Ask people and find out the cost of a cup of tea

★ at a tea stall _____

★ at a hotel _____

> If a person who runs a tea stall earns Rs 30 in a day, how much will he earn in 10 days? _____
>
> And in a month? _____
>
> How did you get the answer? Discuss.

I thought of starting my own business. I thought I should open a bangle shop or a tailor shop. But my uncle said that we could earn a lot by opening a junk shop.

In 2001, my mother-in-law and I opened a junk shop. We took a loan of Rs 8000 for the shop.

Find out: what is a loan?

★ Have you ever heard of someone taking a **loan**? For what? _____

★ How much loan was taken? _____

★ How much money was paid back? _____

Hariya and Babu want to buy a handcart for Rs 300.

> I have taken a loan of Rs 300 from a bank for six months. I will pay Rs 51 every month to the bank.

> But I have taken a loan of Rs 300 from Chunnilal. After six months, I will pay back Rs 360.

Hariya

Babu

Who has to pay back more — Hariya or Babu? _____

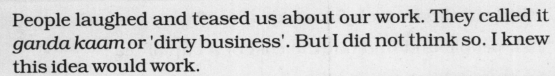

People laughed and teased us about our work. They called it *ganda kaam* or 'dirty business'. But I did not think so. I knew this idea would work.

Now we have a *pucca* house with electricity. We have a fridge, a TV and a gas stove. My husband's brothers, sister and also my daughter go to school.

I have 9 rickshaws of my own. I give the rickshaws on rent, each for Rs 20 a day. On Sundays I do not take any money for them.

How Much does Kiran Earn from 9 Rickshaws in a Day?

For 1 rickshaw she gets Rs 20 per day.

So, for 9 rickshaws she will earn Rs _____.

How did you do it?

> Hey! I will do it like this —
> 9 times 2 is 18.
> So, 9 times 20 is 180.

> But I find this easier.
> For 10 rickshaws she will get
> Rs 20 × 10 = Rs 200.
> So, for 9 rickshaws, she will
> get Rs 200 – ____ = ____ .

Think of some other ways to do it.

Encourage children to use their own strategies to solve such problems. There should be discussion on how they arrived at their answers.

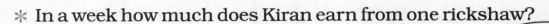

* In a week how much does Kiran earn from one rickshaw?

* **Do it mentally and write the answers.**

2 × 6   = _____   4 × 80 = _____

20 × 6 = _____   4 × 81 = _____

2 × 60 = _____   9 × 25 = _____

3 × 42 = _____   31 × 9 = _____

> 4 × 81 is 4 more than 4 × 80. Am I right?

I have my own small junk shop. I buy junk from junk collectors. They go from house to house and bring junk on handcarts. I then sell it at the big shop.

How Much to Pay for this Junk?

Kiran has bought some junk from junk collectors.

Look up the rate list to see today's rates. Help Kiran to find out the cost of the junk.

> 1 kg newspaper costs Rs 5. 30 kg cost Rs 5 × 30 = Rs 150. So for 31 kg she pays Rs _____.

* How much will Kiran pay for 31 kg newspaper?

This exercise encourages children to use different strategies (other than the standard algorithm) for doing multiplication.

Rate-List

Kind of Junk	Price of 1 Kg
1. Waste Paper	Rs 4/-
2. Newspaper	Rs 5/-
3. Iron	Rs 12/-
4. Brass	Rs 170/-
5. Plastic	Rs 10/-

Can you do this without writing?

* How much will Kiran pay for 42 kg newspaper?

* Also find the cost of:
   a) 22 kg of plastic
   b) 23 kg of waste paper
   c) 12 kg of iron

Guess the total money Kiran will pay to the junk collectors. Will it be
— More than 600?
— Less than 600?

Smart Kiran Sells the Junk

Kiran sells her junk to a big shop. She checks the prices on her mobile phone and sells only when she gets a good price.

Today she has gone to sell plastic, newspaper, iron and brass at Dinu's big shop.

Dinu weighs 32 kg iron, 4 kg brass, 152 kg newspaper, 63 kg plastic.

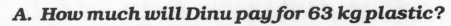

A. How much will Dinu pay for 63 kg plastic?

The rate of 1 kg plastic is Rs 12. So the cost of 63 kg plastic will be Rs 12 × 63.

Remember, you used boxes to multiply two numbers in Class III.

Dinu's Rate-List

Kind of Junk	Price of 1 Kg
1. Newspaper	Rs 6/-
2. Iron	Rs 14/-
3. Brass	Rs 180/-
4. Plastic	Rs 12/-
5. Waste Paper	Rs 4.50/-

	60	3
10	60 × 10 **600**	3 × 10 **30**
2	60 × 2 **120**	3 × 2 **6**

12 × 63 means 12 times 63. 12 times 60 is 720. So, the answer is more than 720. Also the answer is less than 800. Can you tell why?

Dinu added the numbers in the boxes:

```
  600
  120
   30
+   6
─────
  756
```

So, for 63 kg plastic, Dinu will give Rs 756.

✳ Kiran bought 1 kg plastic for Rs 10, but sold 1 kg plastic for Rs 12. How much money does she earn on selling 1 kg plastic? Rs _____

So, how much money does she earn for 63 kg? Rs _____

B. Kiran sells 32 kg iron

✳ How much money will Dinu pay for 32 kg iron?

✳ Kiran buys 1 kg iron for Rs 12, but sells it for Rs 14.

How much does she earn when she sells 32 kg iron? Rs _____

C. What will Dinu pay for 152 kg newspaper?

The rate of 1 kg newspaper is Rs 6. So the cost of 152 kg newspaper is Rs 6 × 152.

Dinu writes:

	100	50	2
6	100 × 6	50 × 6	2×6
	600	**300**	**12**

> 6 × 100 = 600. So, the answer is more than 600. Is the answer less than 1000? How did you guess?

Then he adds the numbers in the boxes:

$$
\begin{array}{r}
600 \\
300 \\
+ \quad 12 \\
\hline
912 \\
\hline
\end{array}
$$

> I bought 1 kg newspaper for Rs 5, but sold it for Rs 6. How much money did I earn by selling 152 kg of newspaper? _____

So, for 152 kg newspaper he will give Kiran Rs 912.

D. What does Dinu pay for brass?

How much money will Dinu pay for 4 kg brass? _____

> Guess the answer first.

First guess the answer and then calculate:

a) $37 \times 18 = 643$

b) $45 \times 24 = 1,080$

c) $69 \times 52 = 3,450$

d) $77 \times 55 = 3,685$

e) $142 \times 5 = 710$

f) $382 \times 3 = 1,116$

g) $2 \times 175 = 350$

h) $4 \times 206 = 824$

Fill My Diary

Kiran bought some junk from the junk collectors. She paid them Rs 841. She sold the junk at Dinu's big shop and Dinu gave her these notes and coins.

6 notes of

3 notes of

8 notes of

7 notes of

4 coins of

6 notes of

Kiran wrote the record in her diary.

	11 March 2007
Money I paid — Rs 841	
Money I got— Rs 600	
— Rs 150	
— Rs 140	
— Rs 60	
— Rs 40	
— Rs 4	
Total Rs 994	
	Rs 994
	– Rs 841
Money I earned :	Rs 153

67

Later she paid Rs 919 to the junk collectors. When she sold the junk she got these notes and coins from Dinu.

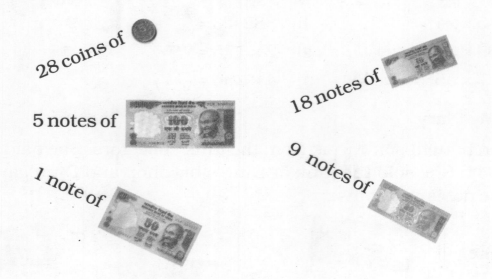

28 coins of

5 notes of

18 notes of

9 notes of

1 note of

Now you make a record in her diary.

Find out how much she earned this time.

18 March 2007

 7 Jugs and Mugs

Bunny and Banno Celebrate their Wedding Anniversary.

Do you remember the wedding in Bunny's family last year? (See Math-Magic Class III page 153). Bunny and Banno decided to have a party one year after their wedding.

They invited their family and friends. They made a special sweet dish — *kheer*.

All the animals came — running, hopping and even crawling!

The elephant is drinking 50 litres of *kheer*.

The giraffe is drinking _____ litres.

The cow is drinking _____ litres.

Then came the squirrel. She said — I can't drink 1 litre of *kheer*, please give me only 500 millilitres.

The donkey asked — 500 millilitres of kheer? Isn't that more than a litre?

The fox said — Come on, don't behave like a donkey! One litre is 1000 millilitres, so 500 millilitres is half a litre.

The frog hopped along with nine other friends. He said — Oh, we only want 100 millilitres each!

OK., here is your *kheer* — said the cat, while serving the *kheer*. She took 10 glasses and poured 100 millilitres *kheer* in each glass.

The donkey looked confused and asked — Ten glasses of 100 mL each. How much is that?

The fox got another chance to show off ! He said — Ah, That is simple! 10 times hundred millilitres is _____ millilitres = _____ litre.

Now you write it   10 × 100 mL = _____ .

Look, a group of ants is marching here! — the grass hopper said.

Are we late?

The *kheer* is finished. Now what can we do? — the cat said sadly.

Don't worry, they won't drink much. Each of them will take only one millilitre. That is all. I will share my *kheer* with them — the elephant said and wiped the cat's tears with his ear.

How many are you all together? — the elephant asked.

We are only one thousand — said the ants.

The cat said — Oh no, one thousand! We have to give *kheer* to 1000 ants!

After thinking the elephant said — No problem, I can manage.

Each ant drinks 1 millilitre of *kheer*.

So, 1000 ants drink: 1000 × 1 mL = _____ mL.

Ah! they will need the same as the ten frogs — said the donkey.

All the ants drank the *kheer*. Everyone was happy. They sang and danced to celebrate the wedding anniversary.

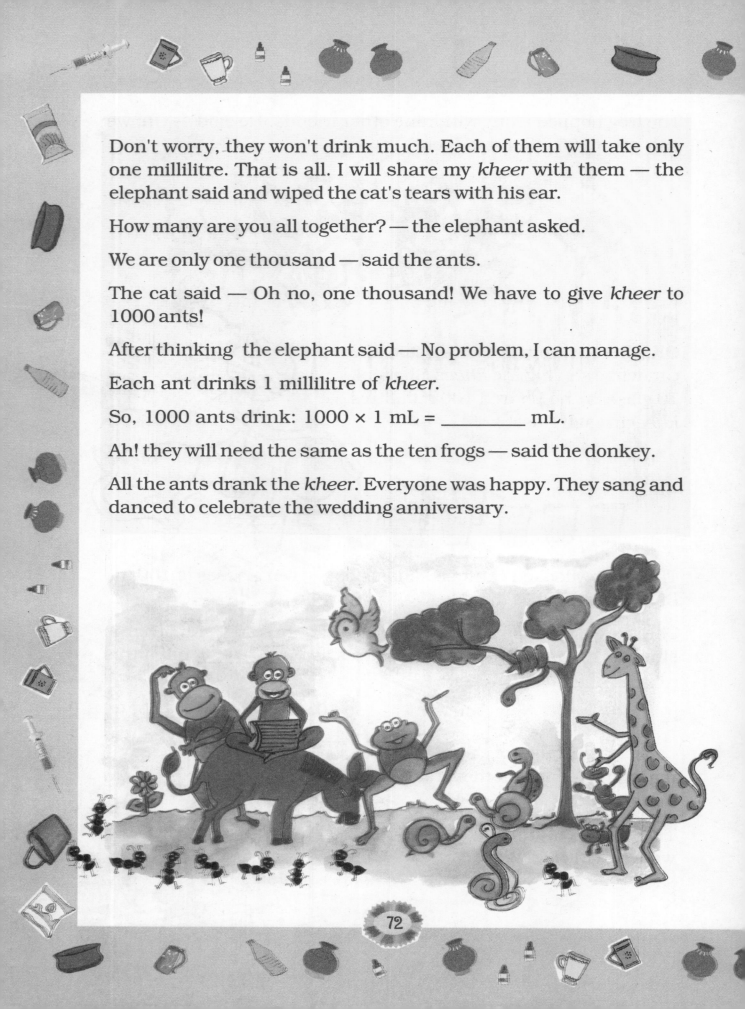

Who can have 1 Litre Kheer

Do you like *kheer*? What do you call it at home?

How much *kheer* can you have?

Can you drink 1 L water at one time?

I think I can drink one litre.

I can drink 400 mL.

The donkey is trying to look for different ways to add up to 1 litre. Help him complete the chart.

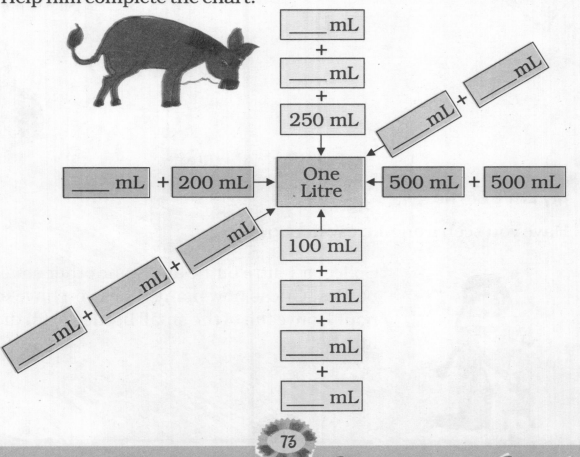

```
_____ mL
   +
_____ mL
   +
 250 mL
   ↓
         _____ mL + _____ mL
                ↘
_____ mL + 200 mL →  One    ← 500 mL + 500 mL
                     Litre
         ↗             ↑
_____ mL + _____ mL + _____ mL
                   100 mL
                     +
                  _____ mL
                     +
                  _____ mL
                     +
                  _____ mL
```

Look Around

Look at these pictures. Now look for some other things we get in packets or bottles like these. Make your own list.

Packet	How many mL or L?
Milk	500 mL

My Litre Bottle

Have you seen a one-litre water bottle?

Collect a 1-litre bottle and some other small bottles. Guess how many times you have to pour from each of the small bottles to fill the litre bottle.

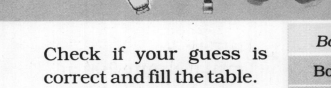

Check if your guess is correct and fill the table.

Bottles	My guess	My measure
Bottle 1		
Bottle 2		
Bottle 3		

Look what Adithyan is saying.

I poured two small bottles of water to fill this 1-litre bottle.

Adithyan

How much water does his small bottle hold?

_____

To fill the 1-litre bottle I need to pour water 5 times from my small bottle.

Leela

Then how much water does Leela's bottle hold? _____

Ramu's Measuring Bottle

Ramu got an empty 250 mL coconut oil bottle. Look at the picture and discuss what he did to make his big measuring bottle.

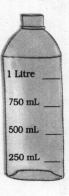

1 Litre ___

750 mL ___

500 mL ___

250 mL ___

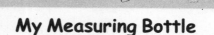

My Measuring Bottle

Find your own way to make a bottle which can measure 200 mL, 400 mL, 600 mL, 800 mL and 1 litre. Discuss with your friends and teacher how you made this.

Guess and check

Look at the buckets, mugs, glasses and other things in your house. Guess how much water each can hold. Check if your guess is right by using your measuring bottle.

	My Guess	My Measure
Mug		
Glass		
Pot		

I think it's a little less than 750 mL.

I think this can carry between 250 mL and 500 mL.

Neetu in Hospital

Neetu has to take 3 injections in a day for 5 days.

How much medicine will she need for one day?

How much medicine in all for 5 days?

One injection gives 5 mL of the medicine to your body.

I am not afraid of injections!

How much medicine will I need for one injection?

How much do we use at a time?

❖ Eye drops   We use less than 1 mL at a time.

❖ _____   _____

❖ _____   _____

❖ _____   _____

List things we use more than one litre at a time.

❖ Water for taking bath

❖ _____

❖ _____

❖ _____

Practice Time

1. Amina's water bottle holds one litre of water. She drank 250 mL of water and her friend Govind drank 150 mL. How much water is left in her bottle?

2. Yusuf runs a tea shop. For making a glass of tea he uses 20 mL of milk. Yesterday he made 100 glasses of tea. How much milk did he use?

3. Radha's grandma was ill. The doctor gave her a bottle with 200 mL of medicine. She has to take the medicine every morning for 10 days.

   How many millilitres of medicine does she have to take every morning? _____

Water- Water

The table shows the water used in one day by a family of 5 people. They live in Goodallur village.

Activity	Water in litres (L)
Cooking and drinking	30 L
Washing clothes	40 L
Cleaning pots, pans	20 L
Bathing	75 L

Total water used by them _____

How many litres of water does your family use in a day? Guess and fill in this table.

Activity	Water used (in buckets)	Water used (in litres)
Cooking and drinking		
Washing clothes		
Cleaning pots, pans		

Drops and Drops Make an Ocean

Is there any tap in your school or your home which is leaking?

How much water do you think we waste through a leaking tap?

Place your litre jar below the leaking tap so as to catch all the drops in the bottle. Note the time. After one hour check how much water is in the bottle.

Find out how much water is wasted in a day. _____

In a week? _____

In a month? _____

In a year? _____

Puzzle

At the Milk Society

Chelannur village has a milk society. Geetha and Ammini went there to buy 4 litres of milk. But the man could not find the one litre measure. He had only a 3 litre and a 5 litre bottle with him. But he gave them exactly 4 litres of milk.

Explain how he did this.

8 Carts & Wheels

Hey! See, how big this wheel is! I have never seen a wheel like this.

You must have seen many such round things around you.

List some more in your notebook.

Carts & Wheels

You must have seen many such round things around you.

> I cannot wear these bangles. These are too small.

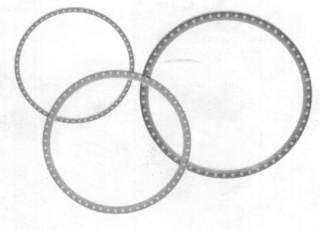

List some more in your notebook.

Round Bangle

Have you ever gone to a bangle shop?

* Guess which of these bangles is of your size.

* Take a wire and make a bangle for yourself. Can your madam or mother wear this bangle? _____

* A bangle can be used to trace a circle. What are the other things around you that you can use to trace a circle?

_____ _____

_____ _____

* Trace a circle with the help of some of these in your notebook

Games with Circles

Children are playing some games ....

Game 1

Game 2

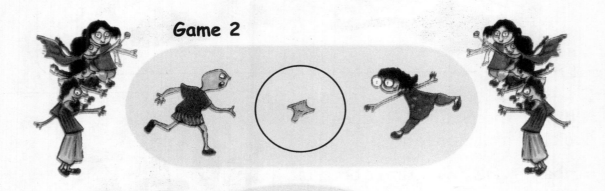

Do you play these games?

Which song do you sing when you play these?

Play these games in your school.

Why do we make a circle in each of these games?

What if a rectangle was made? Discuss.

＊ Think of some other games you play by making circles.

Making a Circle

Naina, Chippu and Ariba want to play a game. They want to make a big circle on the ground. But they cannot make it by tracing. So, Ariba tries to draw a circle with a stick.

Chippu and Naina — It does not look like a circle at all.

Ariba — OK! Why don't both of you try?

Chippu and Naina both make circles on the ground.

✳ Is any of these a good drawing of a circle? Discuss.

✳ Can you draw a circle on the floor with a chalk? Try.

✳ Also draw a circle in your notebook using a pencil.

✳ Look at the circles drawn by your friends. Who has drawn the best circle?

The purpose of this exercise is to give opportunities to each child to make freehand circles. They can also make circles on the ground with a stick. They can compare different drawings to get an intuitive sense of the shape of a circle.

Making a Circle with a Rope

Ariba decided to use nails and a thread to make a circle on the ground. She took a thin rope and tied nails on both ends of the rope. Then she made a circle with the help of her friend. Look at the picture and see how they are making the circle.

Can you also make a circle with a rope and nails like Ariba?

✳ Do the activity in small groups. Each group should take a rope of a different length. See the circles made by different groups.

✳ Which group made the smallest circle? _____

How long was their rope? _____

✳ Does a longer rope make a bigger circle? _____

Can you say why?

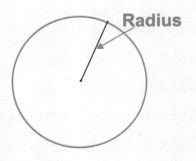

The length of rope used is equal to the length of the **radius** of the circle.

Radius

✳ What was the radius of the smallest circle? _____

The purpose of this exercise is to help children make different circles, measure the lengths of their radii and see how the size of a circle changes with its radius.

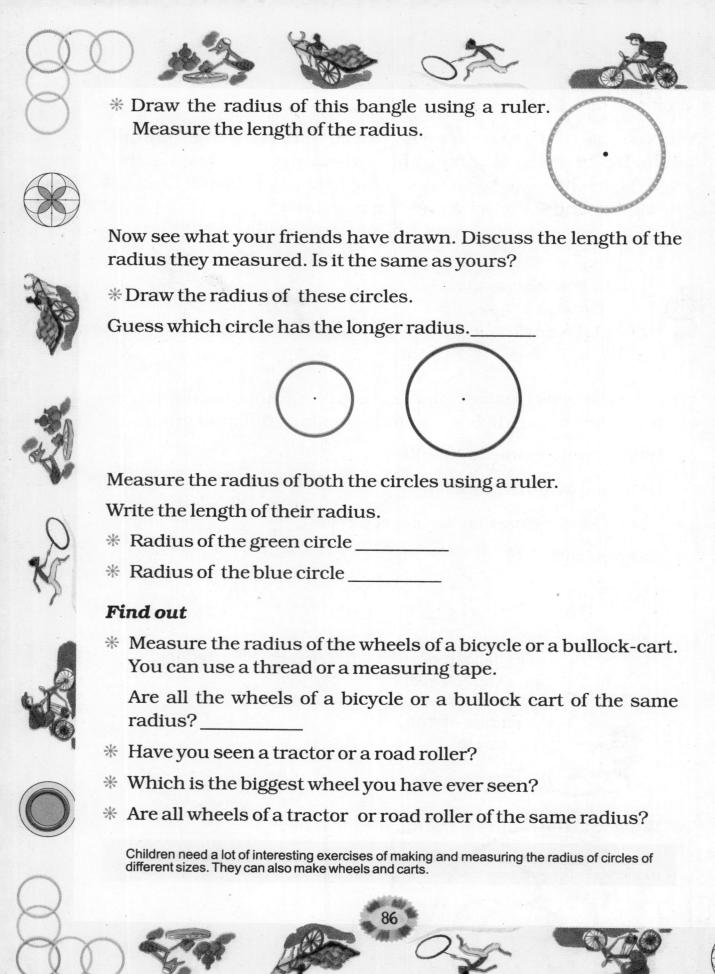

✳ Draw the radius of this bangle using a ruler. Measure the length of the radius.

Now see what your friends have drawn. Discuss the length of the radius they measured. Is it the same as yours?

✳ Draw the radius of these circles.

Guess which circle has the longer radius._____

Measure the radius of both the circles using a ruler.

Write the length of their radius.

✳ Radius of the green circle _____

✳ Radius of the blue circle _____

Find out

✳ Measure the radius of the wheels of a bicycle or a bullock-cart. You can use a thread or a measuring tape.

Are all the wheels of a bicycle or a bullock cart of the same radius? _____

✳ Have you seen a tractor or a road roller?

✳ Which is the biggest wheel you have ever seen?

✳ Are all wheels of a tractor or road roller of the same radius?

Children need a lot of interesting exercises of making and measuring the radius of circles of different sizes. They can also make wheels and carts.

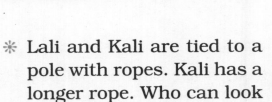

✳ Lali and Kali are tied to a pole with ropes. Kali has a longer rope. Who can look for more grass to eat?

_____

Daljeet's Design

Daljeet has made these designs using a compass.

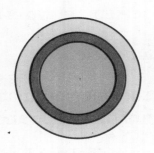
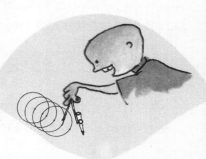

His sister came and started making more designs with him.

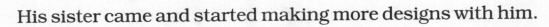

Do you want to make such designs?

To make such designs you will need to use a compass.

Using a Compass

✳ Have you seen a compass before? How will you use this to make a circle?

— Open your compass.

— Press the tip of the compass on the paper. Hold the compass from the top.

— Without moving the tip, try to move the pencil around.

— Do you get a circle?

Look for a mark where you had kept the tip of the compass.

This mark is the **centre** of your circle.

✳ Is this circle better than the one you made earlier without a compass? Draw the radius of this circle and measure it.

✳ Now you can make your own designs like Daljeet had made. How many did you make?

Guess how this design has been made. Use a compass to make a similar one in the box.

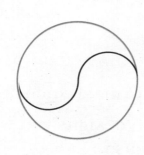

Encourage children to explore their own designs with a compass. This will also give them more practice in drawing circles with a compass.

Is It a Circle?

Naina was making a circle.

Ravi asked her for an eraser. She kept her compass and gave him the eraser. Then she started again to complete her circle. But she got this.

Guess

✳ Why did Naina get such a drawing? Discuss.

Can a circle have more than one centre?

Another day Naina was using a compass to make circle. But it came out like this.

✳ Did any one of you ever get a shape like Naina's?

Oh! The screw of the compass is loose .... Let me tighten it .... Now my compass will not slip ......

89

Find the Centre

Sadiq and Sameena want to make circles for themselves.

I will make it with a compass.

No, I will trace it with a bangle.

Then they cut their circle.

See, my circle has a centre. But where is the centre of your circle?

Don't worry. See how I find it.

She folded her circle into half.

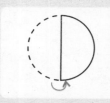

Then she folded it again like this.

She opened the folded circle.

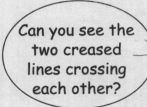

Can you see the two creased lines crossing each other?

Yes

See, I put a point where these lines cross. This is the centre of my circle.

✳ Now you trace a circle on a paper using a bangle. Cut it. Then find its centre like Sameena did.

We can also make the design on page 88 like this. How did you do it?

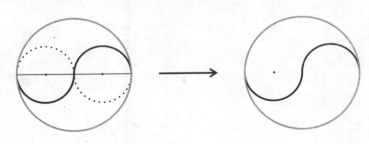

 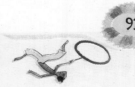   

Balancing Act

Can you balance a plate on your finger?

I will balance it ...

Oops!...
I will try again.

I think I have found the centre of the plate.

You also try to balance a plate or a round lid on your finger. Where does it balance?

Spin the Top

Zakir, Appu, Naina and Guddo were getting bored. It was raining. So they could not go out to play.

Suddenly Appu said — Let's each make a top.

They took a piece of cardboard and traced a circle on it. Then they made a hole and put a matchstick in it.

Now everybody was excited to spin their tops which looked like this.

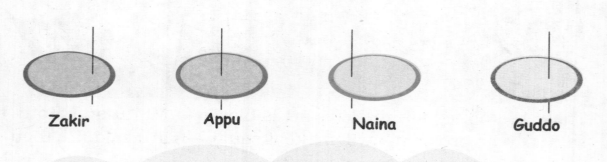

Zakir   Appu   Naina   Guddo

Guess

* Whose top will not spin at all? _____
* Whose top will spin a little? _____
* Whose top will spin the best? _____
* In whose top is the stick nearest to the centre? _____

Make Your Own Top

You also make your own top and play this game.

* To make the top spin well, where will you make the hole?

9 Halves and Quarters

Mintu cat and Mottu cat were friends. Once they stole a chapati from Malini's kitchen. I will take it — said Mintu. No, I will take it — said Mottu. While they were quarrelling, there came Tittu Monkey. Hi! What is the problem? why are you quarrelling? — he asked. "We don't know how to divide this chapati between us — the cats said. OK! don't worry. I will divide the chapati equally for both of you — he said. Clever Tittu divided the chapati like this:

These are not equal, the left part is bigger — Mintu and Mottu said. Oh, no problem, I will make it equal — Tittu said. He then cut a part of the left piece and ate it.

Oh! Now the right part is bigger — the cats cried. I am sorry — said Tittu. He cut a part from the bigger piece and ate it. When there was only a small piece remaining, he said — This is my share for the work. Tittu then quickly ate the last piece and climbed the tree.

Half-Half

❀ If the cats ask you to divide the chapati equally, how will you divide it?

If you do not cheat like Tittu, the cats will have these parts.

Half of Half

❀ If two more cats come for food, how will you divide one chapati equally for four cats?

Each of us got a quarter of the chapati. You are a good 'divider'. Ha!

Half of Many Pieces

Rani got a chocolate. She divided it equally and gave half to her friend Reena.

❀ Circle the portion that Reena got.

How many pieces of chocolate are there? _____

How many pieces were left with Rani? _____

Ha! Half a chocolate is as tasty as a whole chocolate!

Many Shapes from a Half Sheet

Take a piece of paper. Cut the sheet into two equal triangles so that each triangle is equal to half of the sheet.

Shade the two triangles with different colours.

✤ Draw different shapes using these triangles. One such shape is shown here.

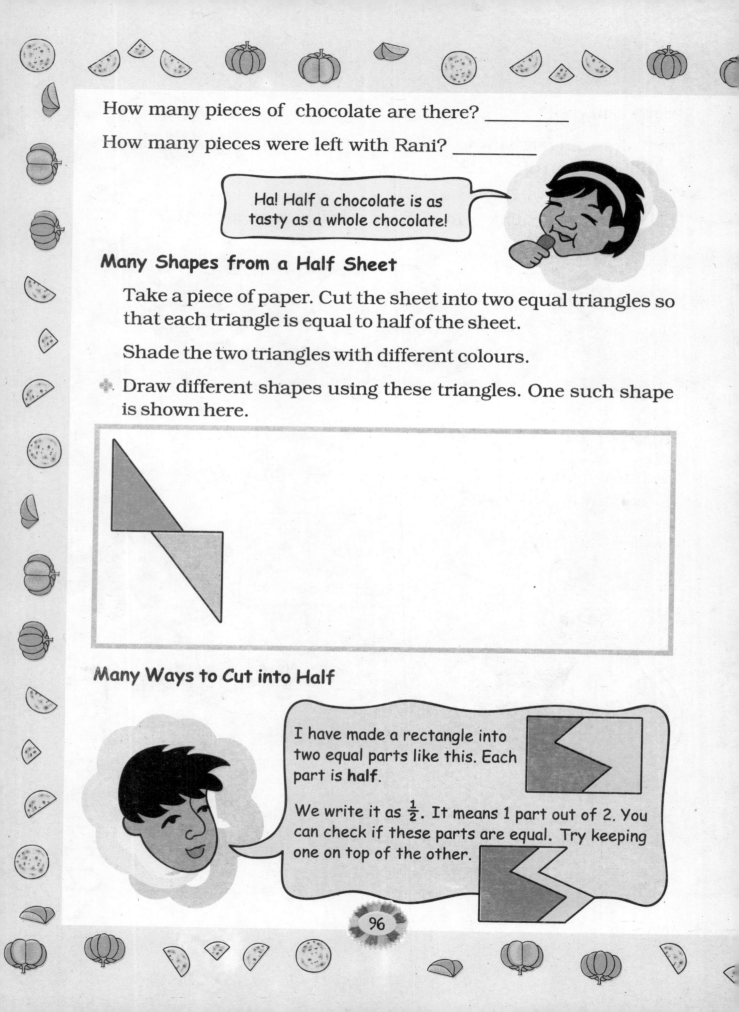

Many Ways to Cut into Half

I have made a rectangle into two equal parts like this. Each part is **half**.

We write it as $\frac{1}{2}$. It means 1 part out of 2. You can check if these parts are equal. Try keeping one on top of the other.

In how many different ways can you cut a **rectangle** into half?

❖ Draw 5 different ways .

Can you check if they are equal?

Many Ways to Make Quarters

I make four parts like this.
Each part is a **quarter**.
And I can write it as $\frac{1}{4}$.
It means 1 part out of 4.

❖ In how many different ways can you cut a rectangle into four
equal parts? Draw 5 different ways.

Can you check if they are equal?

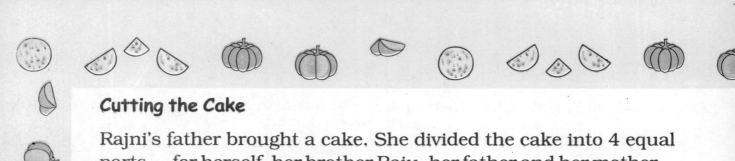

Cutting the Cake

Rajni's father brought a cake. She divided the cake into 4 equal parts — for herself, her brother Raju, her father and her mother.

* Colour each share with different colours.
* How much does each get? _____

* Mother gave her share of cake to Rajni. Now colour the total part that Rajni will get.

* Out of 4 parts Rajni will get _____ parts, which is equal to half of the cake.

So she can write it as $\dfrac{}{4}$ or $\dfrac{1}{2}$.

Before Rajni's mother gave her share to Rajni, she had only $\dfrac{1}{2}$ of 'half the cake', which was $\dfrac{1}{4}$ of the total cake.

* Colour the share Raju got.

* How much of the cake do Rajni and Raju together get? Colour their total share.

Altogether they get 3 parts out of 4, so we can write it as $\dfrac{3}{4}$.

Greedy Kundu

Kundu is a greedy man. Whenever he goes to the market, he wants to get more and more but doesn't want to spend much money.

One day he wants to eat pumpkin *halwa* (sweet dish). He tries to buy a big pumpkin with only Rs10. He asks the first pumpkin seller the price of a big pumpkin.

First pumpkin-seller — $\frac{1}{4}$ of this pumpkin is for Rs 10.

✤ This full pumpkin will cost Rs _____.

Kundu — Eh! For Rs 10, you should give me $\frac{1}{2}$ of this pumpkin.

First pumpkin-seller — Then you go to the next seller, he can give you $\frac{1}{2}$ of such a big pumpkin for Rs 10. I keep only good quality pumpkins.

Kundu walks to the next seller and looks for a pumpkin of the same size.

Kundu — How much of this pumpkin will I get for Rs10?

Second pumpkin-seller — Half.

✤ This full pumpkin will cost Rs _____.

Kundu— Eh! Why not give me $\frac{3}{4}$?

Second pumpkin-seller — Run away! Go, get your pumpkin from that man. He sells such bad vegetables that he will even give you a full pumpkin of this size for Rs 10.

The greedy Kundu walks to the next pumpkin seller. He looks at a pumpkin of the same size and asks him —will you give me this big one for Rs 10?

Third pumpkin-seller — Why don't you climb the roof of that house? You can get pumpkins free from the plant itself!

Kundu is very happy. He climbs the roof of that house and then ....

Using a Price List

a) How much does $\frac{1}{2}$ kg of tomatoes cost?

b) Which costs more – $\frac{1}{2}$ kg of onions or $\frac{1}{4}$ kg of carrots?

c) What is the price of $\frac{3}{4}$ kg of potatoes?

d) Keerthi is going for shopping. She has only Rs 20 with her. Can she buy all the things in her shopping list?

e) Make two questions yourself from the price list.

1.

2.

Item	Price in Rs (per kg)
Tomato	8
Potato	12
Onion	10
Carrot	16
Pumpkin	4

Potato- $\frac{1}{2}$ kg
Pumpkin-2 kg
Carrot- $\frac{1}{4}$ kg

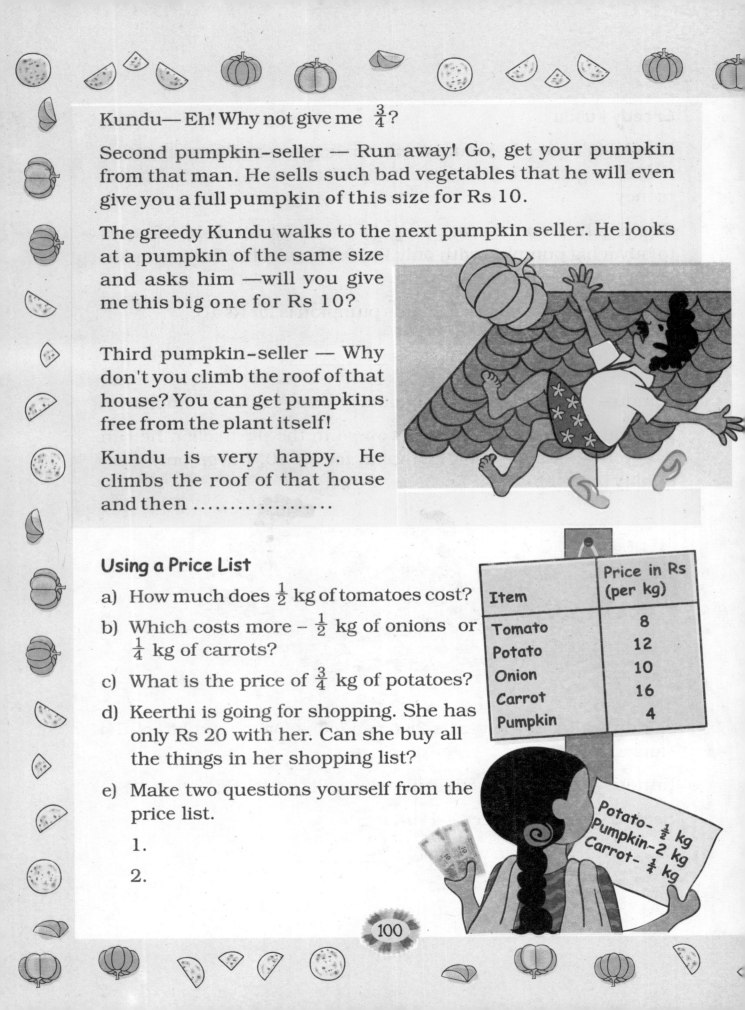

Practice Time

a) What part of the whole is coloured? Write below each shape.

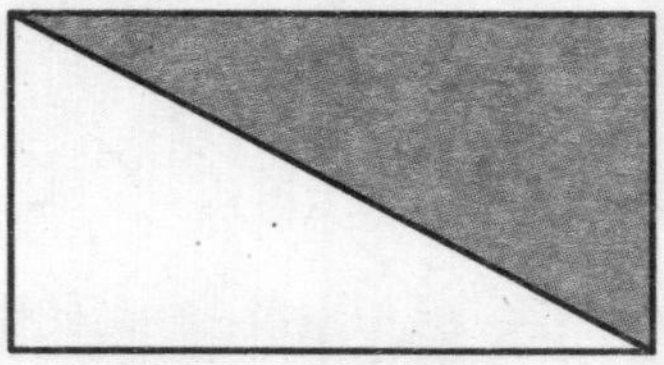

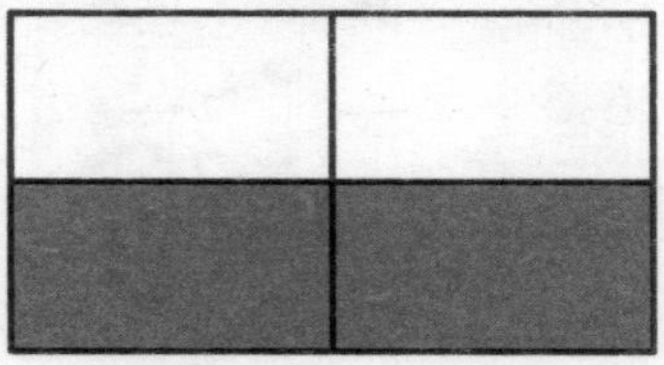

_____   _____

b) Colour that part of the shape which is written below.

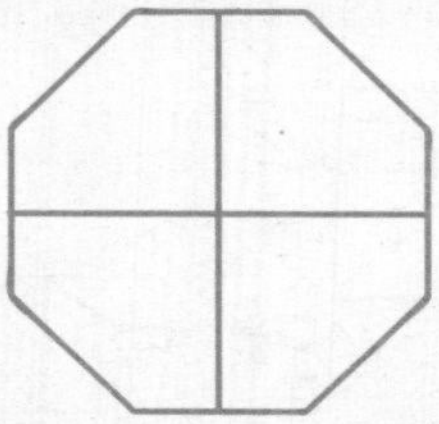

$\frac{1}{2}$

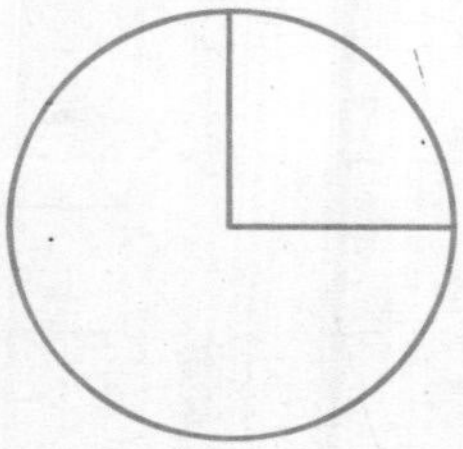

$\frac{3}{4}$

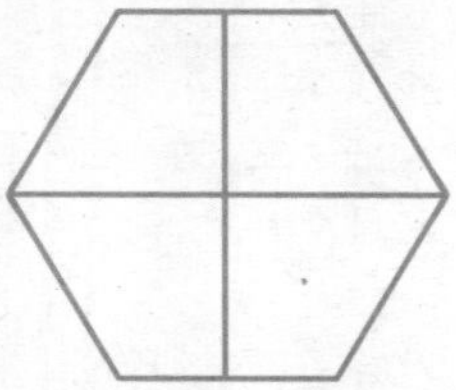

$\frac{3}{4}$

$\frac{1}{4}$

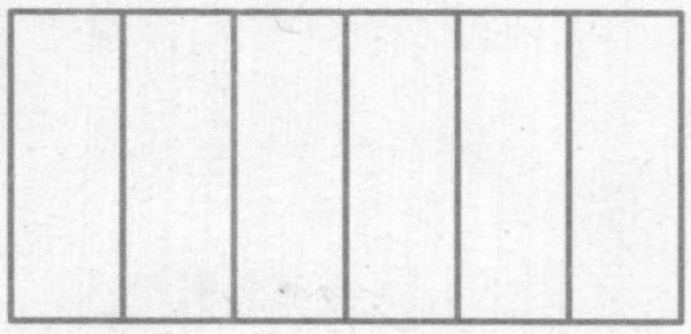

$\frac{1}{2}$

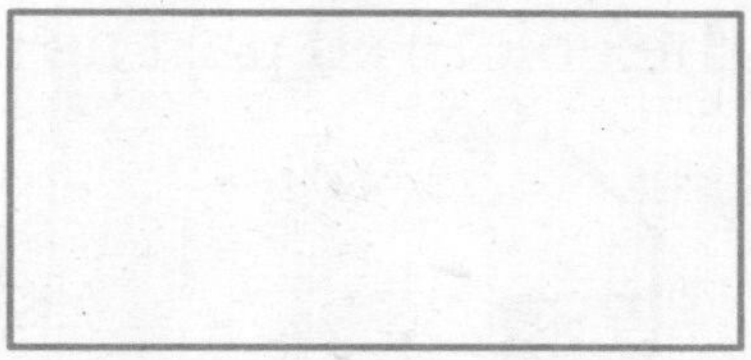

$\frac{3}{4}$

c) *Cut in half*

Draw a line which divides these shapes into half.

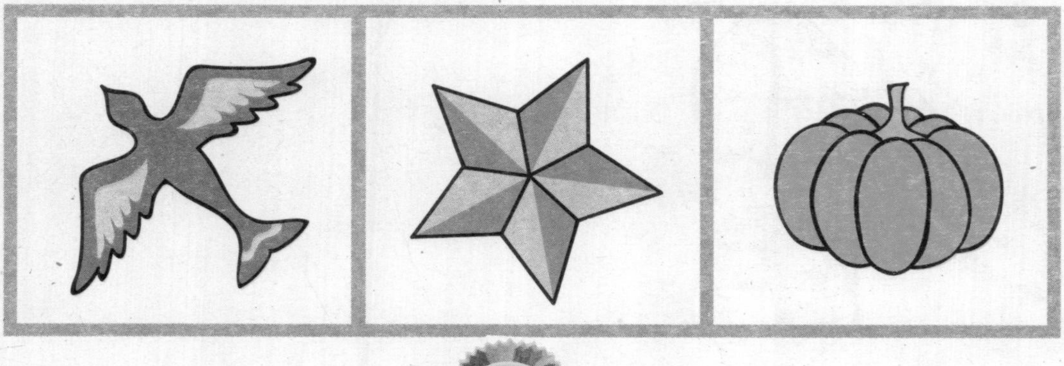

d) Colour half the number of shapes as shown here.

e) Colour $\frac{1}{4}$ of these shapes.

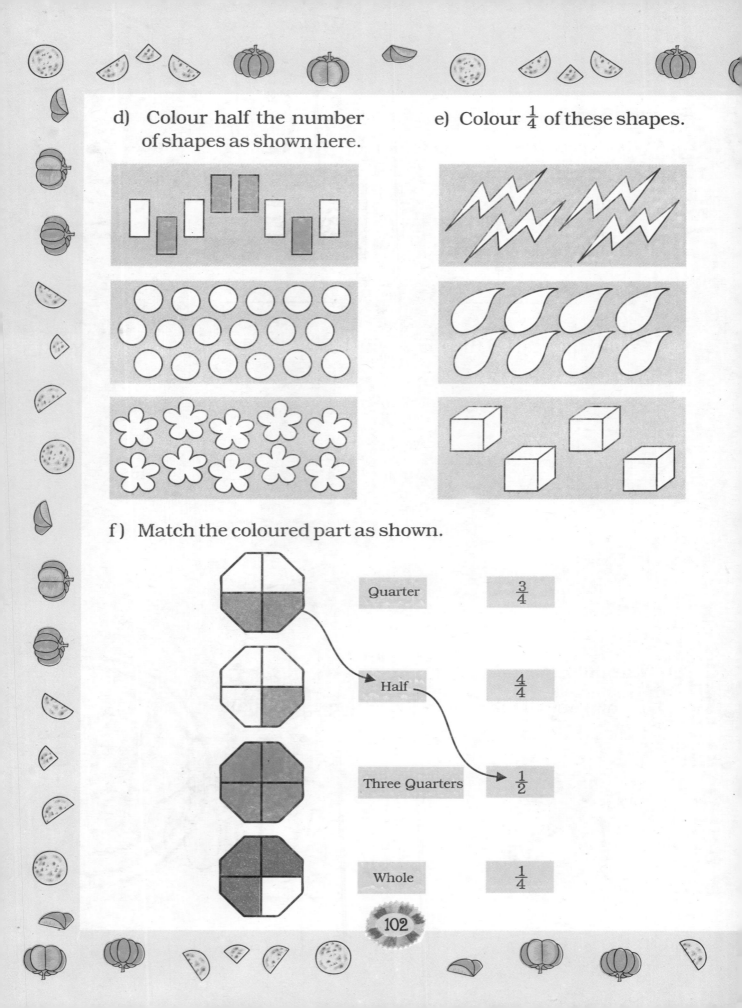

f) Match the coloured part as shown.

Quarter $\frac{3}{4}$

Half $\frac{4}{4}$

Three Quarters $\frac{1}{2}$

Whole $\frac{1}{4}$

g) **Make the other half**

$\frac{1}{2}$ of the picture is drawn here. Can you complete the picture by drawing the other half?

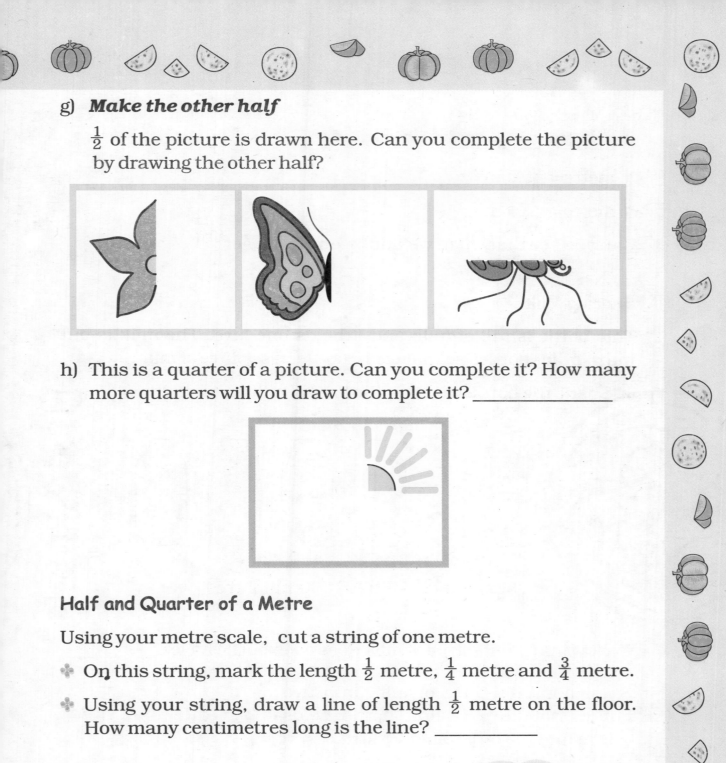

h) This is a quarter of a picture. Can you complete it? How many more quarters will you draw to complete it? _____

Half and Quarter of a Metre

Using your metre scale, cut a string of one metre.

❖ On this string, mark the length $\frac{1}{2}$ metre, $\frac{1}{4}$ metre and $\frac{3}{4}$ metre.

❖ Using your string, draw a line of length $\frac{1}{2}$ metre on the floor. How many centimetres long is the line? _____

Remember,
1 metre = 100 cm

So

$\frac{1}{2}$ metre= ......cm

$\frac{1}{4}$ metre= ......cm

$\frac{3}{4}$ metre= ......cm

Can you see that when we add $\frac{1}{2}$ and $\frac{1}{4}$ we get $\frac{3}{4}$?

Sharing Milk

This bottle is full of milk and it holds one litre. The milk is put into 4 other bottles so that each bottle has $\frac{1}{4}$ litre of milk.

❀ Shade the bottles to show the level of milk in each.

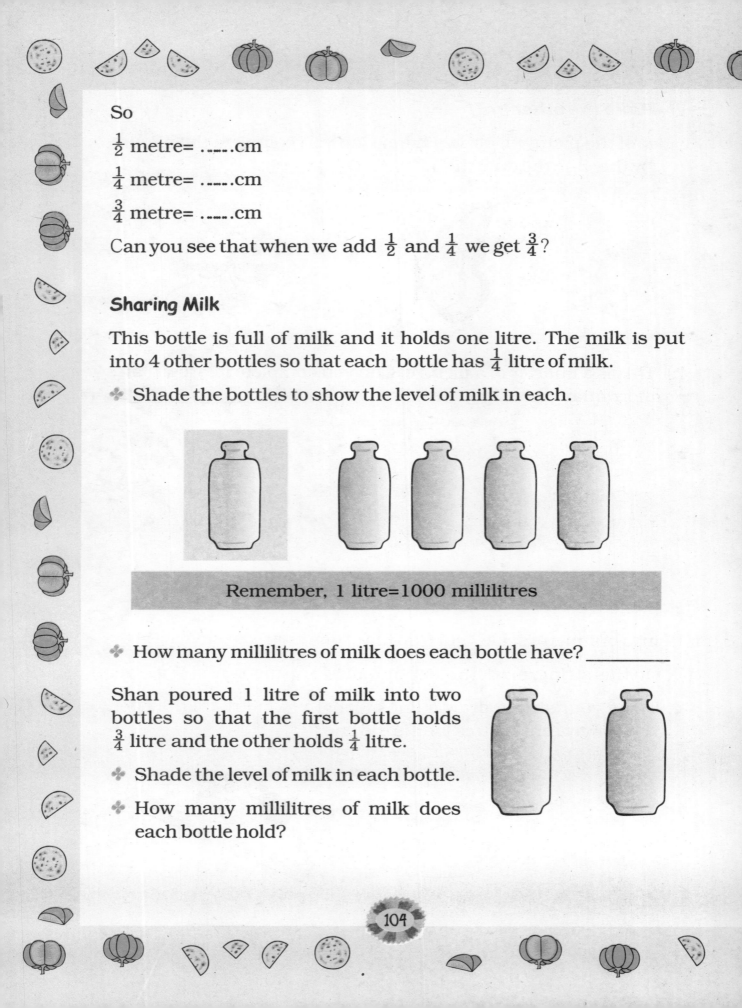

Remember, 1 litre=1000 millilitres

❀ How many millilitres of milk does each bottle have? _____

Shan poured 1 litre of milk into two bottles so that the first bottle holds $\frac{3}{4}$ litre and the other holds $\frac{1}{4}$ litre.

❀ Shade the level of milk in each bottle.

❀ How many millilitres of milk does each bottle hold?

104

Balance the Weight

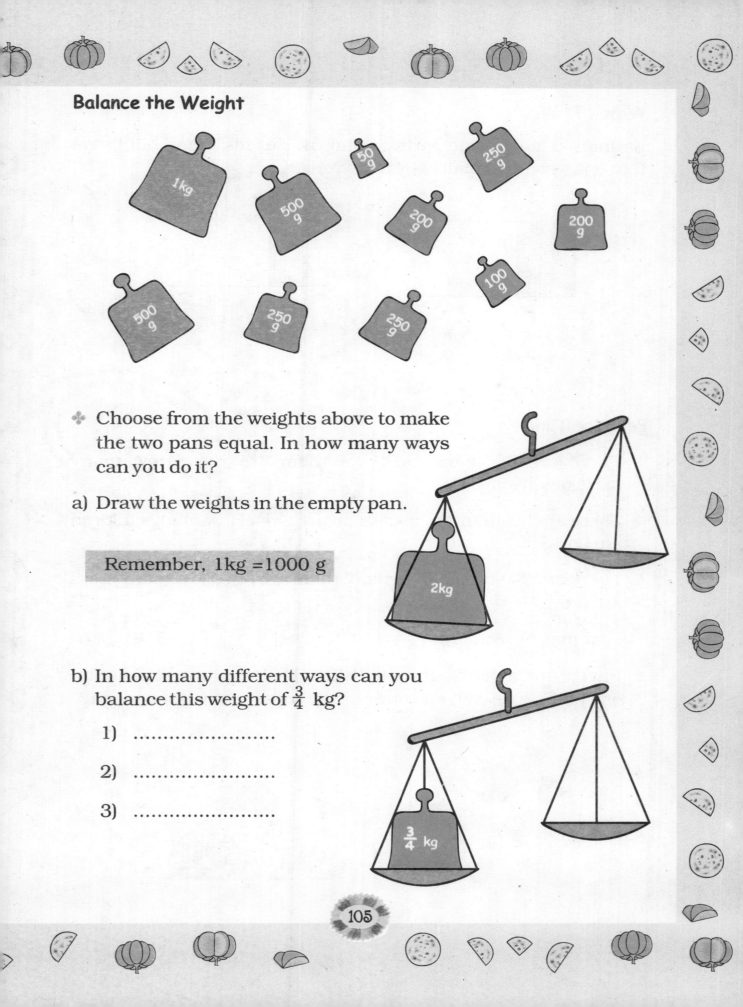

❖ Choose from the weights above to make the two pans equal. In how many ways can you do it?

a) Draw the weights in the empty pan.

> Remember, 1kg =1000 g

b) In how many different ways can you balance this weight of $\frac{3}{4}$ kg?

1) ....

2) ....

3) ....

Why is It Wrong?

Kannan shaded some parts as shown. But his friend Mini says that it is wrong. Explain why it is wrong.

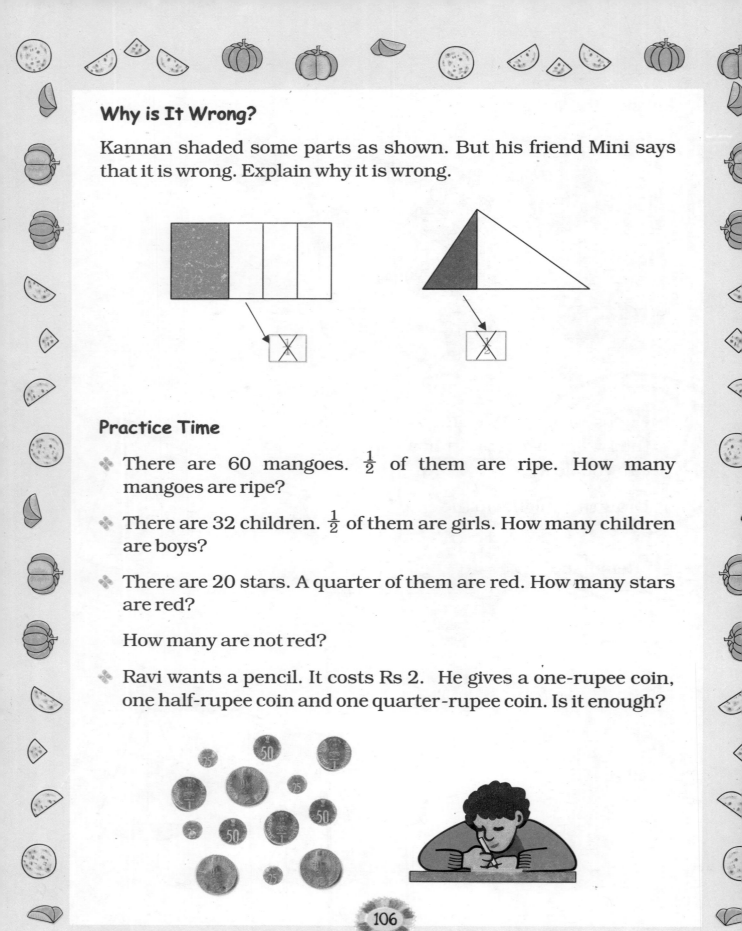

Practice Time

❖ There are 60 mangoes. $\frac{1}{2}$ of them are ripe. How many mangoes are ripe?

❖ There are 32 children. $\frac{1}{2}$ of them are girls. How many children are boys?

❖ There are 20 stars. A quarter of them are red. How many stars are red?

How many are not red?

❖ Ravi wants a pencil. It costs Rs 2. He gives a one-rupee coin, one half-rupee coin and one quarter-rupee coin. Is it enough?

⑩ Play with Patterns

Tinu used this block 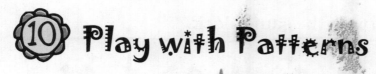 to make a sari.

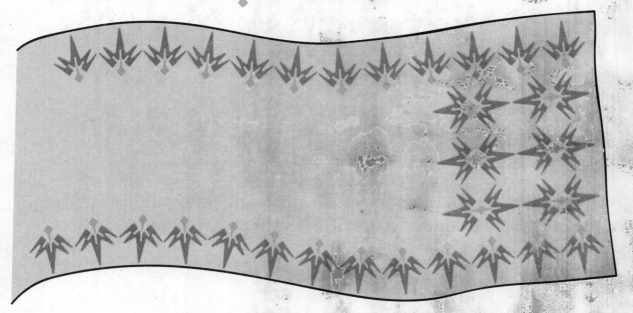

Next he made this bedsheet with the same block.

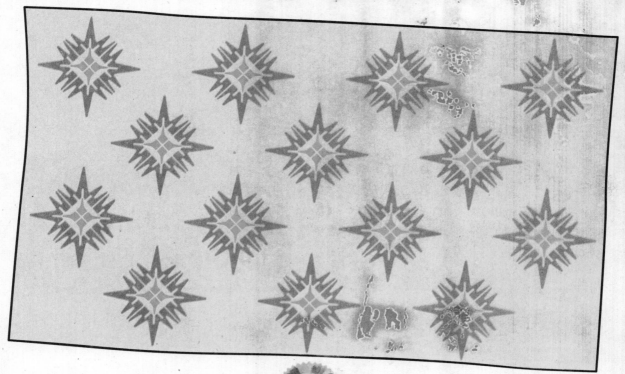

He also made this *dupatta* with the same block.

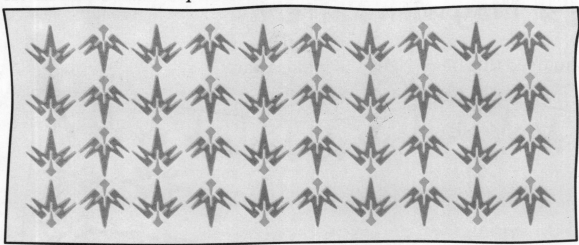

Can you see how Tinu has made different patterns using the same block? Now you too make 3 different patterns using ⚇.

Pattern 1

Pattern 2

Pattern 3

Yamini has used her blocks to make a few patterns. Help her to take these patterns forward.

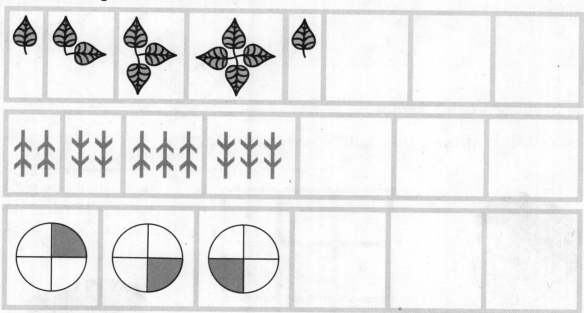

We can also make patterns with numbers and letters. Below are a few examples. Can you take them forward?

| ABC | DEF | GHI | | | |

| 28Z | 27Y | 26X |

| 864 | 764 | 664 |

| 9 | 109 | 209 |

Now write your own number patterns.

Make a pattern without numbers.

No Number Comes Twice

Look at the number box. Can you see a pattern?

1	2	3
3	1	2
2	3	1

No number comes twice in any line!

Now you try writing the letters — A, B, C in the box so that no letter comes twice in any line.

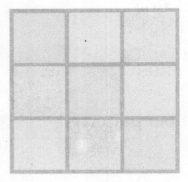

We have not used the terms row or column here, but using the word 'line' teachers may discuss the idea of rows and columns.

Magic Patterns

Look at the pattern of numbers 1 to 7 . See how each line adds up to 12!

Now you fill these stars. Use numbers 1 – 9 and the **rule** that the numbers on each line add up to 15.

Magic Triangles

Look at this number pattern .

Rule: Numbers on each side of the triangle add up to 9.

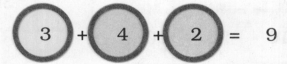

3 + 4 + 2 = 9

See if the other sides of the triangle also add up to 9.

Now use numbers 1 – 6 to make your own magic triangle.

Rule: Numbers on each side must add up to 10.

Number Towers

Numbers can be arranged as a tower. We start from below and get this number pattern.

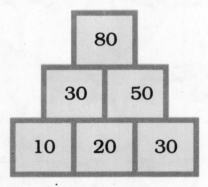

Can you see the rule for this pattern?

Rule: We add 2 numbers below to get the number in the box above them.

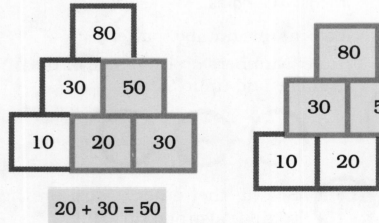

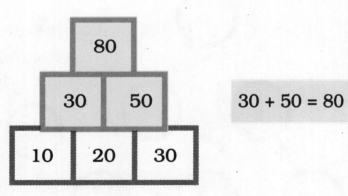

$30 + 50 = 80$

$20 + 30 = 50$

Using the same rule, complete these number towers.

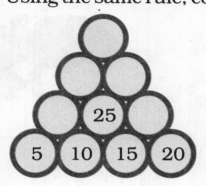

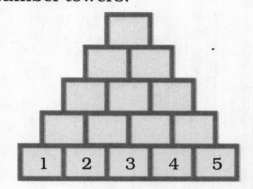

The Same Sum Rule

Some friends are playing with number cards. See how they add.

First from left

First from right

11	+	16	=	27
12	+	15	=	27
13	+	14	=	27

Can you see the rule which gives us the same sum each time?

Rule: We get the same sum when we add the two numbers —

First from left   and   First from right

Second from left   and   Second from right

Third from left   and   Third from right

Now you write any number and the three numbers after that. Make a pattern using the rule.

See if you get the same sum.

	+		=	
	+		=	

24-01-07

Patterns with Addition

$1 + 2 + 3 = 6$

$2 + 3 + 4 = 9$

$3 + 4 + 5 = 12$

Oh! The sum grows by 3 each time.

Here, the sum grows by 4 each time.

$1 + 2 + 3 + 4 = 10$

$2 + 3 + 4 + 5 = 14$

$3 + 4 + 5 + 6 = 18$

Now, you try to make such a pattern with 5 numbers in order.

☐ + ☐ + ☐ + ☐ + ☐ = ☐

☐ + ☐ + ☐ + ☐ = ☐

☐ + ☐ + ☐ + ☐ = ☐

☐ + ☐ + ☐ + ☐ = ☐

☐ + ☐ + ☐ + ☐ = ☐

Does the sum grow by 5 each time?

Secret Messages

Yamini explained the rule — Numbers have been used for letters.

For example, 'J' is 10, 'P' is 16. So (JUMP) is (10 21 13 16).

✳ Complete this list of letters and numbers to help you.

A	B	C	D	E	F	G	H	I	J	K	L	M	N	O	P	Q	R	S	T	U	V	W	X	Y	Z
1	2	3	4	5	6	7	8	9	10	11	12	13	14	15	16	17	18	19	20	21	22	23	24	25	26

✳ Teenu wants to write to his friend 'Good Morning'.

What will he write by using the same rule?

✳ If we change the rule and write 1 in place of 'B', 3 in place of 'D' and so on, then how will we write 'Let Us Dance'?

Coding and decoding secret messages is also a part of recognising patterns. Recognising rules is important for the development of mathematical thinking.

More Secret Messages

Shablu and Jaggu are playing a game. They are writing some secret messages. But Kahuli is not able to understand them. So Jaggu explained the rule —

Jaggu –   You see, we have changed each letter by its next letter. That is, we write 'G' in place of 'F', 'O' in place of 'N'. So YES becomes ZFT.

Kahuli – Oh! Now I understand.

Kahuli – See what I have written   XF BSF GSJFOE T

✳ What was Kahuli's secret message? _____

✳ What did Shablu and Jaggu write?

_____

✳ Use the same rule to write — 'Meet me on the moon'.

_____

✳ Make different rules and ask your friends to crack the secret message.

Upside Down

Anisha is playing. She is showing her friends that she can stand on her head.

Now, Anisha is playing with this card. Draw what it will look like when upside down.

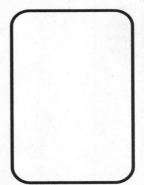

Floor Patterns

Have you ever seen a floor with tiles of these shapes?

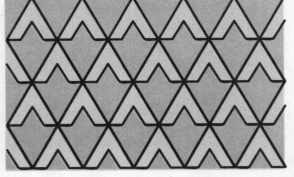

These designs are made by covering the floor completely with tiles that fit into each other without any gaps.

a) Now, you cover this floor with this tile.

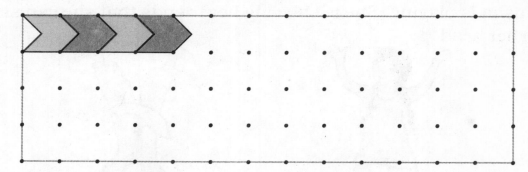

Can you make such a floor design with a tile like a circle?

b) Try with this green tile without leaving a gap. Could you do it? Discuss with your friends.

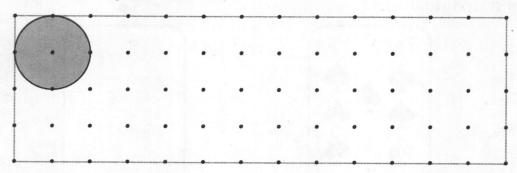

c) Complete this tiling pattern.

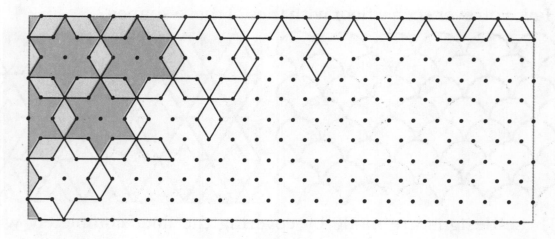

d) Ramaiya has made a wall with his blocks. Can you complete this for him?

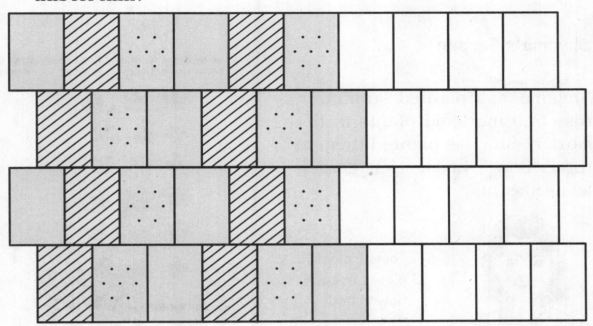

e) Renu began to paint this wall. Now you help her to complete it.

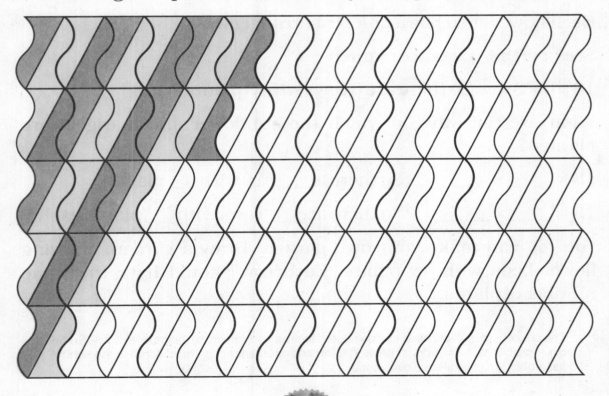

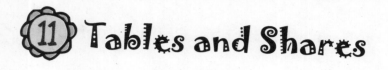

11 Tables and Shares

Shyama's Garden

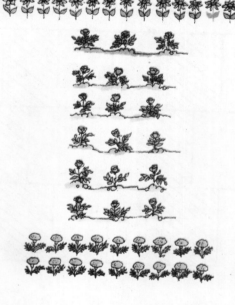

Shyama has planted sunflower, rose and marigold plants in her garden. She has planted them in three flower-beds. Her garden looks like this.

See, how I planted 18 plants in each flower bed!

Each flower-bed has a different arrangement.

See how the roses are planted.

$18 = 6 \times 3$ So there are 6 rows with 3 plants each.

What are the ways in which the sunflower and marigold are planted?

$18 = $ _____ $\times$ _____   So there is ___ row with ___ plants.

$18 = $ _____ $\times$ _____   So there are ___ rows with ___ plants each.

You too can make your own garden. Draw a garden, showing flower-beds with 48 plants. Each row should have the same number of plants.

The concept of multiplication can be related to the arrangement of things in an array. Some other problems, based on contexts like the arrangement of chairs, children in the school assembly, etc., can also be discussed.

Jars in the Shelf

Bheema made a shelf for 30 jars. This is a long shelf with two rows. Each row has the same number of jars.

Can you think of other ways to make a shelf to keep 30 jars?

* Draw a shelf. Show how many jars you will keep in each row. How many rows are there?

Have your friends drawn it in different ways?

Easy Tricks

I do not know the multiplication table of 7.

Bunty

I know the tables till 5 but there is an easy trick.

I can make the table of 7 with the tables of 2 and 5.

Guddu

Children will enjoy building new multiplication tables for themselves instead of only memorising them.

Table of 2

1×2	2×2	3×2	4×2	5×2	6×2	7×2	8×2	9×2	10×2
2	4	6	8	10	12	14	16	18	20

Table of 5

1×5	2×5	3×5	4×5	5×5	6×5	7×5	8×5	9×5	10×5
5	10	15	20	25	30	35	40	45	50

Table of 7

7	14	21	28	35	42	49	56	63	70

See, how I added the two numbers in the yellow boxes to get the table of 7.

Aha... it is easy. I can also make the table of 7 with the tables of 4 and 3.

Help Bunty to make the table of 7, using tables of 4 and 3.

Table of 4

1×4	2×4	3×4	4×4	5×4	6×4	7×4	8×4	9×4	10×4
4	8								

Table of 3

1×3	2×3	3×3	4×3	5×3	6×3	7×3	8×3	9×3	10×3
3	6								

Table of 7

7									

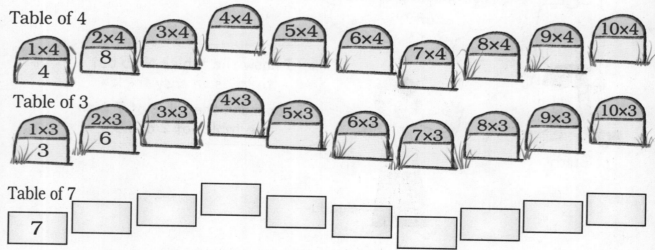

Which two tables will you use for writing the table of 12?

122

How Many Cats?

Some of Gayatri's cats were playing in a box. When she tried to count, all she could see were legs. She counted 28 legs. How many cats are there in the box?

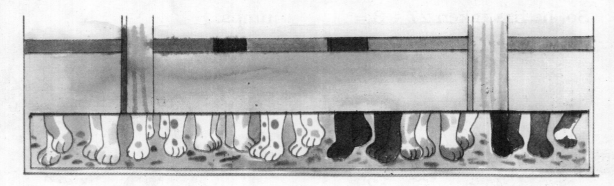

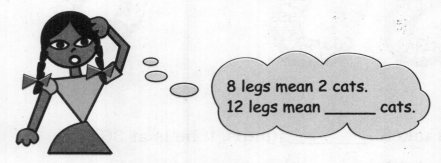

8 legs mean 2 cats.
12 legs mean _____ cats.

How many legs?	4	8	12					
How many cats?	1	2						

So 28 legs mean _____ cats.

* Billo has kept his chickens in a box. He counted 28 legs. How many chickens are there?

* Leela has not gone to school for 21 days. For how many weeks was she away from school?

Encourage children to fill in the table and also proceed towards making generalisations. For example, they should be able to see that 48 legs would mean there are 12 cats, or vice versa. In fact, this forms the foundation for algebraic thinking in later years.

Jumping Animals

Do you remember the jumping animals of Class III?

A **frog** jumps 3 steps at a time starting from 0.

✳ Count the jumps he takes to reach 27.

So, he has taken 27 ÷ 3 = _____ jumps.

✳ He has taken _____ jumps, if he is at 36.

✳ If he is at 42, he has taken _____ jumps.

Starting from 0, a **rabbit** jumps 5 steps at a time.

✳ In how many jumps does he reach 25? _____

✳ He reaches _____ after taking 8 jumps.

✳ He needs _____ jumps to reach 55.

Practice Time

1) 28 ÷ 2 =	2) 56 ÷ 7 =
3) 48 ÷ 4 =	4) 66 ÷ 6 =
5) 96 ÷ 8 =	6) 110 ÷ 10 =

Children have done similar kinds of exercises for multiplication and division in Class III. Refer to pages 173-176, Math-Magic Class III, NCERT.

Sea Shells

Dhruv lives near the sea. He thought of making necklaces for his three friends. He looked for sea-shells the whole day. He collected 112 sea-shells by evening. Now he had many different colourful and shiny shells.

I will make a necklace of 28 shells. Will these shells be enough to make necklaces for all my friends?

He took 28 shells for one necklace.

112 – 28 = 84

Now he was left with 84 shells. Again he took 28 more shells for the second necklace.

✳ How many shells are left now? _____

Then he took shells for the third necklace.

✳ So he was left with _____ shells.

✳ How many necklaces can Dhruv make from 112 shells? _____

✳ Are the shells enough for making necklaces for all his friends? _____

Try these

A) Kannu made a necklace of 17 sea-shells. How many such necklaces can be made using 100 sea-shells?

Encourage children to solve questions based on division with large numbers, for which they do not know multiplication tables, using repeated subtraction. More problems based on real life contexts can be given.

B) One carton can hold 85 soap bars. Shally wants to pack 338 soap bars. How many cartons does she need for packing all of them?

C) Manpreet wants 1500 sacks of cement for making a house. A truck carries 250 sacks at a time. How many trips will the truck make?

A driver charges Rs 500 for a trip. How much will Manpreet pay the driver for all the trips?

Gangu's Sweets

Gangu is making sweets for Id. He has made a tray of 80 *laddoos*.

Please pack 4 laddoos in a box. I need 23 small boxes.

Rabiya

∗ Are the sweets in the tray enough to pack 23 small boxes?

_____

∗ How many more sweets are needed? _____

> For solving this problem, encourage children to use their own strategies — of making groups in the tray, using multiplication to do division or repeated subtraction, etc.

✳ Gangu also has a bigger box in which he packs 12 *laddoos*. How many boxes does he need for packing 60 *laddoos*?

Practice Time

1) Neelu brought 15 storybooks to her class. Today 45 students are present. How many children will need to share one book?

2) A family of 8 people needs 60 kg wheat for a month. How much wheat does this family need for a week?

3) Razia wants change for Rs 500.

How many notes will she get if she wants in return —

(a) All 100 rupee notes? _____

(b) All 50 rupee notes? _____

(c) All 20 rupee notes? _____

(d) All 5 rupee notes? _____

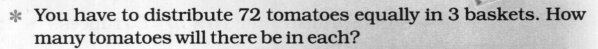

✳ You have to distribute 72 tomatoes equally in 3 baskets. How many tomatoes will there be in each?

✳ There are 350 bricks in a hand-cart. Binod found the weight of a brick to be 2 kg. What will be the weight of all the bricks?

Children and their Grandfather

Rashi, Seema, Mridul, Rohit and Lokesh asked their grandfather to give them money for the Fair.

> I have 70 rupees in my pocket. Tell me how to share money equally among all of you . If you are right, you get this money!

One method

Rashi and Seema thought for a while and said — We know how to do 70 ÷ 5.

Seema starts writing and says —

$$
\begin{array}{r}
10 \\
5\overline{)\ 70} \\
-\ 50 \\
\hline
20
\end{array}
$$

→ First I give Rs 10 to each one of us.

→ So, I have distributed 5 × 10 = 50 rupees.

→ 20 rupees are still left.

Rashi completes it like this. She says —

$$
\begin{array}{r}
10 + 4 \\
5\overline{)\ 70} \\
-\ 50 \\
\hline
20 \\
-\ 20 \\
\hline
0
\end{array}
$$

I give 4 rupees more to each. So I have distributed 20 rupees.

Now nothing is left. And all the money is divided equally.

So, each gets 10 + 4 = 14 rupees.

This method is actually about how children divide when they distribute some objects repeatedly. In this case, they might first give Rs 10 each to five people and then next distribute the remaining money in the second round. They could as well distribute it by first giving Rs 5 to each. Children can, thus, use any way to complete the process of division. This is the beauty of this method.

Another Method

Mridul and Lokesh are trying 70 ÷ 5 in a different way.

Lokesh writes —

First, I give Rs 5 to each. $\longrightarrow$

I have distributed 5 × 5 = 25 rupees. $\longrightarrow$

Next, I give Rs 6 more to every one.

I have distributed 30 rupees more. $\longrightarrow$

Now I am left with _____ rupees. $\longrightarrow$

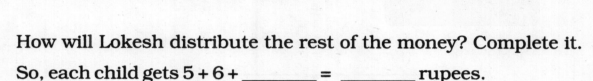

$$
\begin{array}{r}
5 + 6 \\
5 \overline{)\ 70} \\
-\ 25 \\
\hline
45 \\
-\ 30 \\
\hline
? \\
\end{array}
$$

How will Lokesh distribute the rest of the money? Complete it.

So, each child gets 5 + 6 + _____ = _____ rupees.

Check your answer!
Multiply your answer by 5 and
see if you get 70. Is your
answer correct?

Your Method

* Now use your own method to divide Rs 70 equally among
  5 people. If you want you can start by giving Rs 2 to each.
  Or you can even start with Rs 11 to each.

Can you start with
Rs 15 to each?

Try Doing These

a) $5 \overline{)\ 65}$

b) 84 ÷ 2

c) $3 \overline{)\ 69}$

d) 90 ÷ 6

e) $4 \overline{)\ 72}$

f) $9 \overline{)\ 108}$

g) 232 ÷ 2

h) $2 \overline{)\ 428}$

i) Meera made 204 candles to sell in the market. She makes packets of 6. How many packets will she make?

If she packs them in packets of 12, then how many packets will she make?

j) On Sports Day, 161 children are in the school playground. They are standing in 7 equal rows. How many children are there in each row?

Story Problems

Srishti's grandma is asking her to make problems.

Look at the picture and make a question on it.

There are 3 crates. Each crate has 24 bottles in it.

My question: How many bottles are there in all?

Now you look at the other pictures and make questions like Srishti.

1.

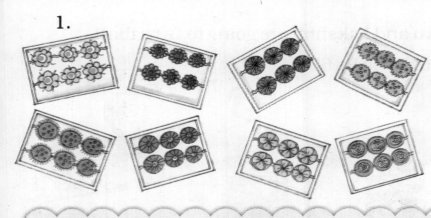

There are 8 packets of *rakhis*.

Each packet has 6 *rakhis* in it.

Your question:

2.

There are 10 packets of sugar.

Saurabh paid 110 rupees for all the packets.

Your question:

3.

There are 35 students in 7 rows. Each row has the same number of students.

Your question:

131

4. Hari, Seema, Chinku and Lakshmi are going to Guwahati.
   The cost of one rail ticket is Rs 62.

Your question:

5. One metre of cloth costs Rs 20. Lalbiak bought some cloth and paid Rs 140.

Your question:

Also guess the answers.

⑫ How Heavy? How Light?

Jaiju and Mannu were shifting house. They loaded all their things on a horse-cart. There were many things like — a water tank, five sacks of wheat, three tables, an almirah, four chairs, two mattresses, three sacks of rice, a bamboo ladder, pots and pans.

When they were ready to move, the horse refused to start. They wondered why. Their father said that this horse was not well and would not pull a load heavier than 700 kg. Oh! But how heavy is this load? — they asked.

Father gave them some idea of the weight of each thing.

Thing loaded	Weight
A sack of wheat	100 kg
A sack of rice	35 kg
Water tank	50 kg
Almirah	70 kg
A table	10 kg
A chair	5 kg
A mattress	20 kg
Bamboo ladder	10 kg
Pots and pans	10 kg

✳ Find out the total weight they had loaded on the cart.

Now they decided to remove a few things from the cart.

✳ Which things should be removed so that the weight of the load is not more than 700 kgs?

_____

_____

The things which were loaded on the cart were big in size and also very heavy. To measure the weight of such heavy and big things, we need a big balance.

But Jaiju and Mannu wanted to make their own balance. They collected a few things — a stick, two lids and a thick thread. They made this balance.

✳ Now you also make your own balance. Write down how you made it. Also draw a picture of your balance in the box below.

Activity

Mannu and Jaiju put a pencil and a geometry box in the two pans of the balance. Which pan will go down? Why? Draw a picture to show it.

What is heavier?

✳ Make pairs of different things and use the balance to decide which is heavier. First guess which thing will take the pan down and then check with your balance.

What is the heaviest?

✳ Make groups of three things. For example — eraser, ball and paper. Use the balance to arrange them in order of weight – the lightest, the one with in-between weight, the heaviest. Complete the table with at least five examples.

Lightest	In-between weight	Heaviest
Paper	Eraser	Ball

✳ Can you find your own weight using this balance?

> The balance children make will not be very accurate but will be good enough to compare weights which are different from each other.

Making Weights

Do this activity in pairs. You need a balance, weights, a cake of soap, plastic packets, sand and rubber bands. You can also take help of an older person.

Get a new cake of soap. The packet will have the weight written on it. You can use this soap to make your own different weights.

The soap weighs _____ grams (g).

Take a small plastic packet.

Put it in one pan of the balance. Put the soap in the other pan.

Slowly add sand to the packet till the pans are balanced.

Close the packet with a rubber band or string. Now stick a strip of paper and write '____ g' on it.

If you put the soap and the weight you just made together in a pan, how many grams will both these weigh? _____

Now make different weights — 150 g, 200 g and 250 g. You can use soaps of different weights for this.

Also make some bigger weights of 500 g, 1000 g, and 750 g.

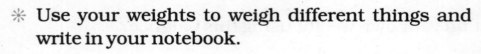

* Use your weights to weigh different things and write in your notebook.

Practice Time

※ **Which pan of the balance will go down? Show by drawing an arrow.**

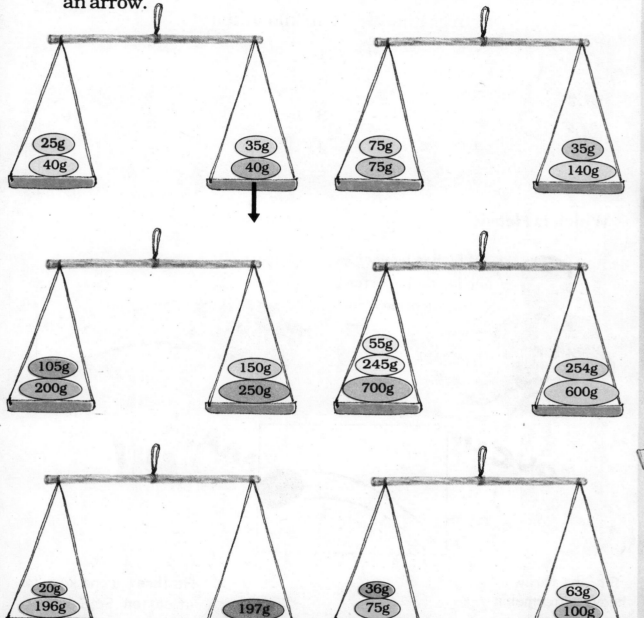

Balance 1	Balance 2
25g / 40g	35g / 40g
75g / 75g	35g / 140g
105g / 200g	150g / 250g
55g / 245g / 700g	254g / 600g
20g / 196g	197g
36g / 75g	63g / 100g

※ **Is the weight on any of the pans equal to 1 kilogram? Mark it.**

※ **How many grams are there in 1 kg?**

137

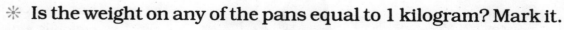

Grams and Kilograms

Name 5 things that we usually buy —

In grams	In kilograms
1.	1.
2.	2.
3.	3.
4.	4.
5.	5.

Which is Heavier?

Which is heavier — one kilogram cotton or one kilogram iron?

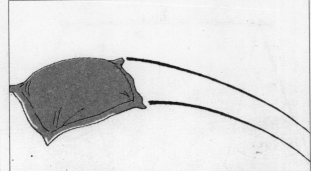

OUCH!

AAA... ...AAH!

Sir, she threw a heavy watermelon at me!

He threw a one kg pillow of cotton. So, I threw a one kg watermelon! Yesterday you said that the weight of 1 kg cotton and 1 kg melon is equal.

Dinesan Went Shopping

Dinesan went to a shop and bought some things.

His younger brother cut the end of the bill where the weights were written.

✳ Guess and write the weight of each thing he bought in g or kg.

Items	Weight	
Rice	5	
Sugar	1	
Mustard seeds	10	
Wheat	3	
Dal	500	
Tea	250	
Pepper	25	

Car and Tractor

Ritu is weighing her toys. She wants to know if her tractor is heavier than her car. How would you help her to find out quickly?

Guess which is the heaviest — a real car, a bus or a tractor?

Which is the heaviest thing you have seen?

If I put 2 cars, will the tractor still be heavier?

Elephant's Weight

Once a king had pain in his stomach. None of the palace doctors could cure his pain.

The king then said:

On hearing this, doctors from all over the country came. But only Dr. Vaidika could cure him.

But, the greedy king didn't want to give her the gold. So, he thought of a trick.

OK, first find the weight of an elephant. Then I will give you that much gold.

Vaidika was unhappy when she reached home. She told her daughter the whole story.

How can I weigh an elephant? Where will I get such a big balance?

Don't worry Ma. I have an idea ..... tell the king to arrange an elephant and a big boat.

Next morning, Dr. Vaidika invited the king near a river. The king came with an elephant and a big boat.

I think she is a fool. How will she weigh an elephant with a boat!

141

Vaidika's daughter went into the river. She marked on the boat how much it sank in the river.

Then she asked them to bring the elephant into the boat. The boat sank deeper. So she marked the new water level on the boat.

Now imagine what happened next and complete the story. Discuss with your friends how Vaidika's daughter found the weight of the elephant.

How Much the Chair Weighs

Anamika wants to weigh this chair using the weighing machine.

Can you suggest a way for doing this?

Broken Stones

Abdu sells firewood. There was a stone in his shop which weighed 13 kg. He used it to weigh firewood.

One day the stone fell down and broke into three pieces which weighed – 2 kg, 5 kg and 6 kg.

5 kg   6 kg   2 kg

But Abdu was very smart. He used those three pieces to weigh firewood of all weights — from 1 kg to 9 kg.

Here is how Abdu weighed 1 kg of firewood —

Ah! The weight of this bundle is 1 kg.

5 kg   6 kg

♣ Now you show how Abdu will use these stone pieces to weigh —

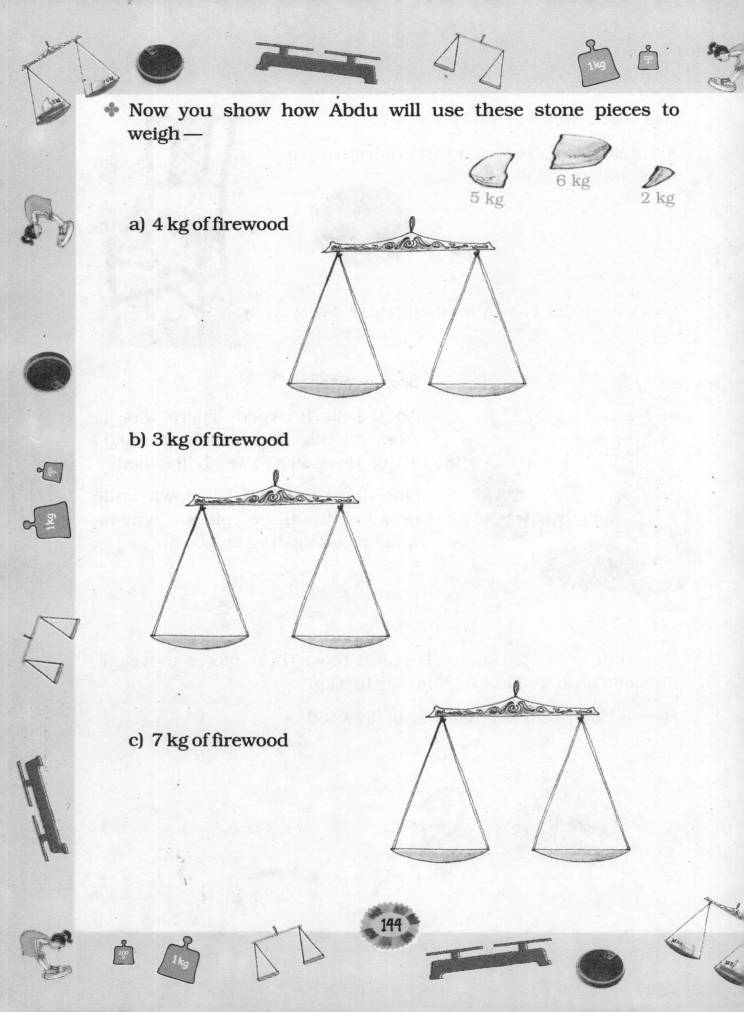

5 kg

6 kg

2 kg

a) 4 kg of firewood

b) 3 kg of firewood

c) 7 kg of firewood

Post Office

Have you ever been to a post office? _____

What different things do people go there for?

How much does a postcard cost? _____

How much does an inland letter cost? _____

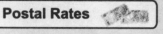

Postal Items	Postal Rates (in Rs)
Single post card	0.50
Printed post card	6.00
Inland Letter	2.50
Letter weighing – i) 20 grams or less ii) For every additional 20 grams	5.00 2.00
Parcel weighing – i) 50 grams or less ii) For every additional 50 grams	5.00 3.00

भारतीय डाक INDIA POST — **Postal Rates**

Look at the postal rates given in the chart.

1. How much will you have to pay for stamps on a letter weighing 50 grams? _____

2. Akash wants to send a parcel of the Math Magic textbook to his friend Rani in Chennai. The book weighs 200 g. See the chart to find the cost of posting the book. _____

3. Read the weight shown in the picture. Find out the cost of sending a parcel of that weight.

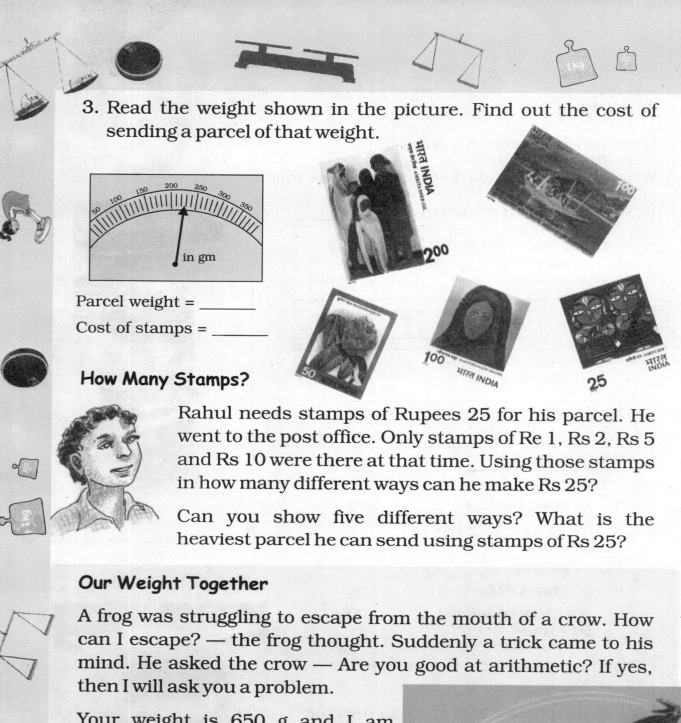

Parcel weight = _____

Cost of stamps = _____

How Many Stamps?

Rahul needs stamps of Rupees 25 for his parcel. He went to the post office. Only stamps of Re 1, Rs 2, Rs 5 and Rs 10 were there at that time. Using those stamps in how many different ways can he make Rs 25?

Can you show five different ways? What is the heaviest parcel he can send using stamps of Rs 25?

Our Weight Together

A frog was struggling to escape from the mouth of a crow. How can I escape? — the frog thought. Suddenly a trick came to his mind. He asked the crow — Are you good at arithmetic? If yes, then I will ask you a problem.

Your weight is 650 g and I am only 145 g. How much do we weigh together?

The crow was good at mathematics, so he happily opened his beak to answer.

What happened after that? So what was the answer the crow wanted to give? _____

146

Am I Fit or Fat?

The chart shows the height and weight of children between 6 and 10 years old.

Name	Age	Height	Weight
Temshula	6	3 feet, 7 inches	16 kg
Sreekunth	10	4 feet, 3 inches	23 kg
Rabiya	6	3 feet, 10 inches	17 kg
Vineet	8	3 feet, 11 inches	19.5 kg
Kavita	9	3 feet, 10 inches	20 kg

Now, you also fill the table by finding out the age, height and weight of any five friends.

Name	Age	Height	Weight

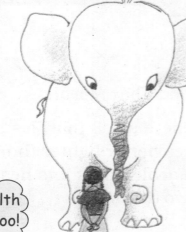

Can you make my health chart?

My health chart too!

Puzzle

How Many Oranges?

All oranges have equal weight. The two papayas have the same weight. The weights in the first and second balances are equal.

How many oranges balance the weight in the third?

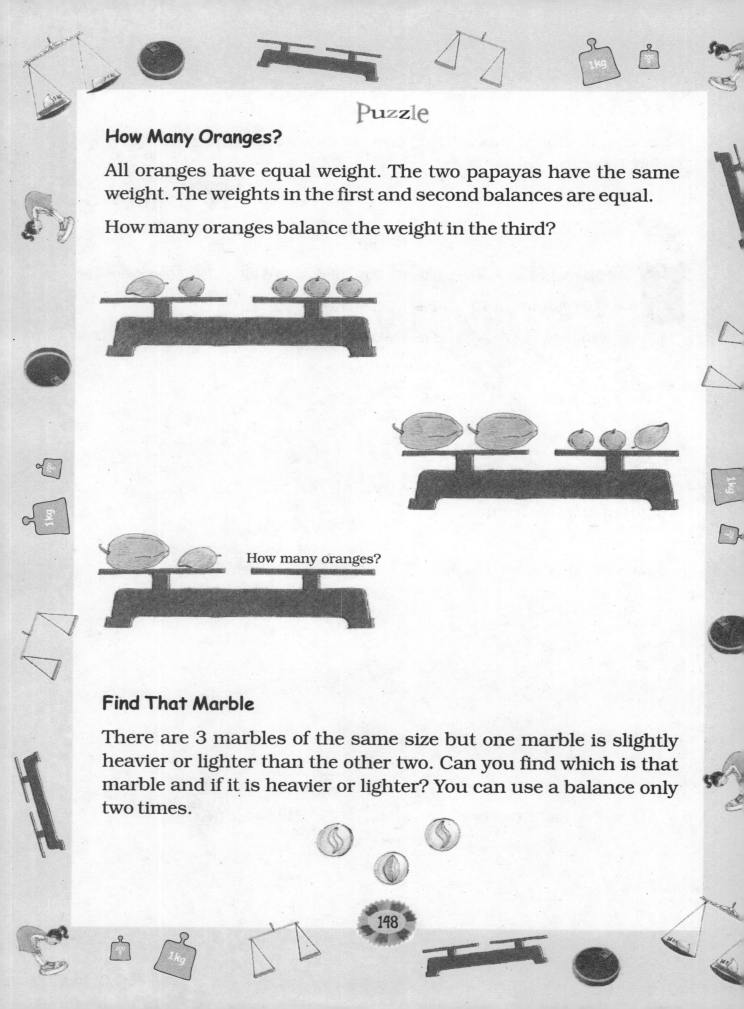

How many oranges?

Find That Marble

There are 3 marbles of the same size but one marble is slightly heavier or lighter than the other two. Can you find which is that marble and if it is heavier or lighter? You can use a balance only two times.

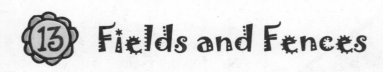

13 Fields and Fences

Rahmat is a farmer. He grows wheat in his field.

I need a fence around my field. How much wire should I buy?

Rahmat needs to find the length of the boundary of the field. Can you find it from this picture? See the length of each side written near it.

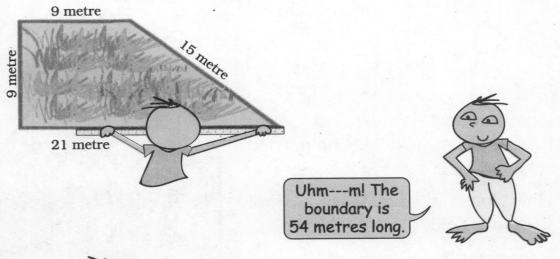

9 metre

9 metre

15 metre

21 metre

Uhm---m! The boundary is 54 metres long.

Rahmat bought a roll of 70 m wire for the fence.

How much wire did Rahmat give to Ganpat? _____

Ganpat thanked Rahmat and started fencing his own field. But he needed to get more wire.

✳ How long is the boundary of Ganpat's field? _____

✳ How much more wire will Ganpat need for his field? _____

Practice Time

1. Here are pictures of some more fields. Find out which one has the longest boundary.

a)

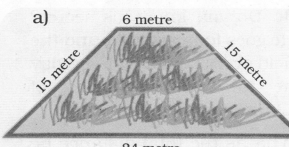

6 metre

15 metre

15 metre

24 metre

Boundary = _____ metre

b)

6 metre

9 metre

3 metre

6 metre

6 metre

12 metre

Boundary = _____ metre

c)

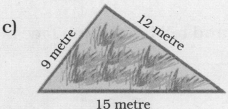

12 metre

9 metre

15 metre

Boundary = _____ metre

d)

9 metre

15 metre

15 metre

15 metre

15 metre

9 metre

Boundary = _____ metre

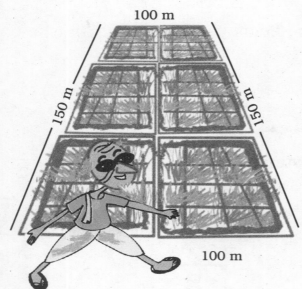

100 m

150 m

150 m

100 m

2. Chandu's father is called the 'young old man' in his village. At 70 years of age, he is fully fit. Do you know his secret? He goes for a walk around the field every morning. Everyday he takes four rounds of Chandu's field.

✳ What is the total distance he covers?

4 × _____ = _____ m = _____ km

3. Ganpat's wife works in a tailor's shop. She has to fix lace around a table cloth.

She bought a 100 metre roll of lace.

✳ Look at the picture of the table cloth and tell how much lace is used for one table cloth. _____

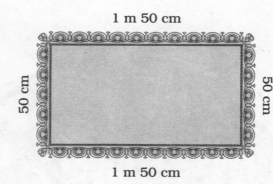

1 m 50 cm

50 cm

50 cm

1 m 50 cm

✳ How much lace will be used in 3 such table cloths? _____
✳ How much lace will be left in the roll? _____

Activity

1. Find out the length of the boundary of these shapes. (Hint :– You can use a thread)

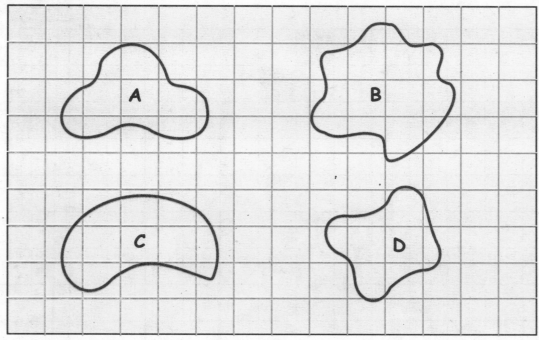

Now count the squares to find out :

✳ How many squares are there in each shape?

✳ Which shape covers the least number of squares?

✳ Which shape covers the most number of squares?

2. Take a 20 centimetre long thread. Make different shapes by joining the ends. Place on the squared sheet on the next page. Find out:

✳ How many squares are there in each shape?

✳ Which is the biggest shape?

✳ Which is the smallest shape?

✳ How long is the boundary of each shape?

Children could be asked to ignore a square if it is less than half, but count it as 1 if is more than half. This will give them a feel for ' rounding off'.

3. How many different shapes can you make by joining two squares? Draw them on the squared sheet given below. How long is the boundary of each shape?

Try this activity with three squares also.

Practice Time

1. A square has a boundary of 12 cm.

a) From the corner of this square, a small square of side 1 cm is cut off. Will the boundary of B be less or more? Find its length.

b) If you cut a 1 cm square to get shape C, what will be the length of the boundary of C?

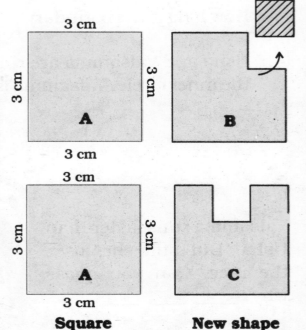

Square   **New shape**

2. a) Find the length of the boundary of square D.

   b) 8 squares of side 1 cm are cut out of the square D. Now it looks like shape E. What is the length of the boundary of shape E?

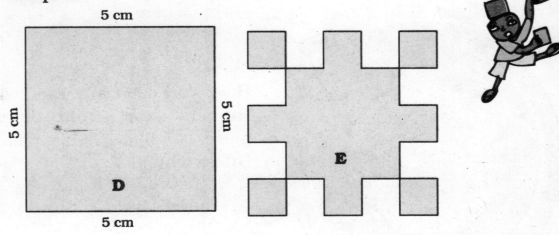

c) The boundary of this is ____ + ____ + ____ + ____

   Can we also say that the boundary is 4 × 1 cm?

155

3. A hockey field is 91 metres 40 cm long and 55 metres wide. How long is the boundary of the field?

4. Usha and Valsamma are running a race. Usha is running on the inner circle. Valsamma is running on the outer circle.

Valsamma runs faster than Usha. But still she loses the race. Can you guess why? _____

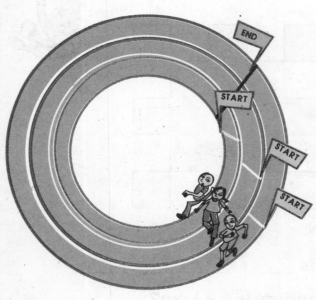

Have you seen any race where runners start from different places — like in this picture? Guess why?

School Garden

The students of Class III and IV thought of making a vegetable garden. They chose a place which looked like this.

Students of both the classes thought that garden 1 was bigger. So both wanted to take garden 1. Suddenly Neetu said

I think both gardens are equally big.

Quite possible! Let us find out if you are right.

✳ How will Neetu find out if the two gardens are equally big?

Activity

1. Look at the table in your classroom. Guess how many Math-Magic books you can place on it.

   (Remember — The books should not overlap. Do not leave gaps between the books.)

   Write your guess here. _____

   Now check if your guess was right. How many books could you place?

   _____

   What is the difference between your guess and the actual number of books? _____

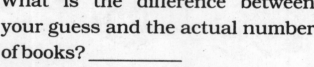

2. Now look for another table.

   a) Is this table bigger than the last table?   Yes/No

   b) Make a guess how many Math-Magic books can be kept on this table. _____

   c) Check if your guess was correct.

      How many Math-Magic books could you keep? _____

   d) The difference between the sizes of the two tables is _____ books.

3. a) How many Math-Magic books can be covered with one sheet of newspaper?

   b) Try covering your Math-Magic book with half a sheet of newspaper.

   c) Can you cover your book with a smaller sheet?

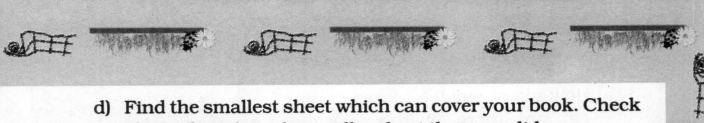

d) Find the smallest sheet which can cover your book. Check if your friend used a smaller sheet than you did.

4. a) Which is the biggest leaf in this picture?

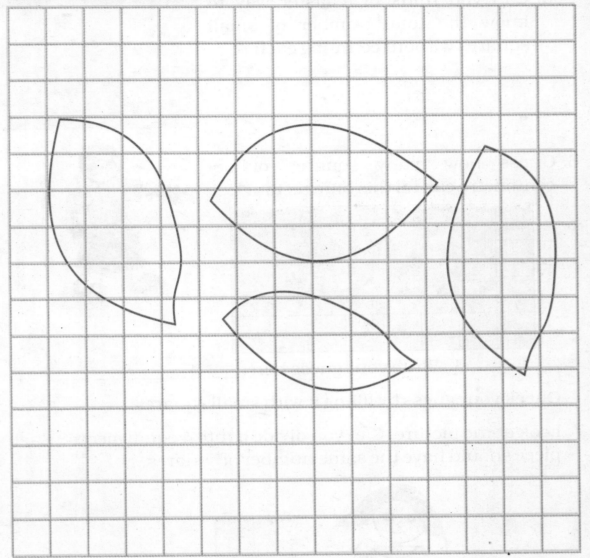

b) Collect some leaves from the garden. Place each of them here on this squared sheet. Trace out their edges and check how many squares there are in each leaf.

c) Which is the biggest leaf?

d) Which is the smallest leaf?

5 . a) How many small squares of size 1 cm are there in this big green square?

b) Can you think of a faster way to know the total number of small squares without counting each ?

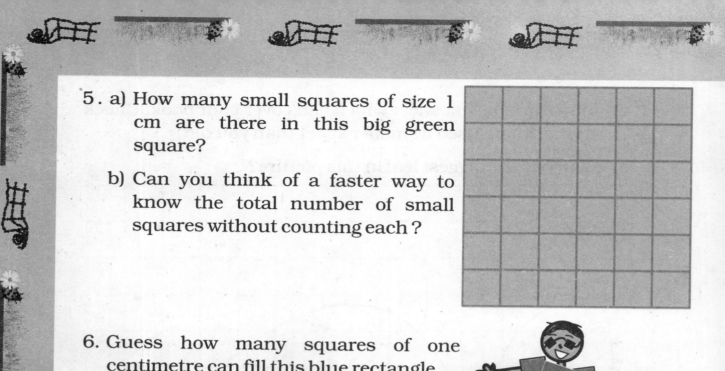

6. Guess how many squares of one centimetre can fill this blue rectangle.

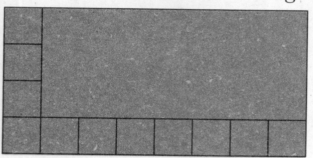

Write your guess here. _____

Check your guess by filling it with small squares.

7. Look at the picture. Can you divide it into 4 equal pieces? Each piece should have the same number of squares.

Puzzle: A House and the Well

Raghavan has a piece of land.

There are 4 houses on his land and in the middle there is a well.
He wants to divide this land equally among his four children.
Each should get one house and be able to use the well without
entering the other's land. Can you help him divide the land?

Give different colours to each one's share.

Smart Charts

How Many Hours?

All of us enjoy watching television (TV) or listening to the radio.

How much time do we spend in this?

❖ Note the time you spend in front of a TV or radio every day. Do this for one week. The time spent in a week is _____ hours.

So in a month you spend about 30 × ___ = _____ hours.

❖ Find out from your friends the time they spend in a week.

How many hours they watch TV or listen to the radio (in a week)	Number of children
More than 6 hours	
Six hours	
Five hours	
Four hours	
Three hours	
Two hours	
One hour	
Zero hour (do not watch)	

I can watch TV for 24 hours! Is it good or bad for me?

From your table

Watching TV/listening to the radio...

❖ _____ children spend more than 6 hours in a week.

❖ _____ children spend no time at all.

❖ Most children spend _____ hours in a week.

❖ _____ children spend more than 3 hours.

Which Programme?

There are different types of programmes on TV or radio such as cartoons, news, sports, music, plays, serials. Juhi's father likes watching serials. Her mother likes sports. Juhi likes news programmes.

(1) Ask people in your family to name one programme they like and one programme they dislike. Make a table.

Family member	Programme they like	Programme they dislike
Mother		
Father		

The kind of programme most family members like _____

The kind of programme most family members dislike _____

2) Find out from 20 friends the programmes they like and dislike, and write in a table.

Kind of programme	Number of children liking it	Number of children disliking it
News		
Serials		
Cartoons		
Comedy shows		
Sports		

❖ Which kind of programme is liked by most children?

❖ Which kind of programme is disliked by the least number of children?

❖ How many children like sports programmes?

❖ Is there any kind of programme not liked by any one? Yes/No If yes, which one? _____.

Who is my friend?

I've a friend with me always,

In the nights and through the days.

When I run he runs with me,

Sometimes I lead, sometimes he.

When it's dark he can't be seen,

Do you know which friend I mean?

❖ Read the poem carefully and answer these questions:

a) Which word comes most often in the poem?

b) Which letter has been used most?

c) Which letter comes the least?

❖ Take a paragraph you like from your language textbook. Read carefully and find out:

a) Which word comes most often? _____
   How many times? _____

b) Which word comes least often? _____

c) The letter used most often is _____

d) The letter used least often is _____

Food We Eat

Children were talking about what things they eat in the morning — made of rice, wheat, maize, barley, etc.

I eat **rice** and things made from rice.

I eat **chapatis** made from wheat.

But, I eat **rotis** made from maize.

I like to drink **sattu** made of barley.

My favourite is **porridge** made from *ragi.*

Find out from your classmates and fill the table:

Main food	Number of persons
Rice	
Wheat	

Look at the table and tell:

❖ Most children eat food made from _____.

❖ Compared to children who eat rice, those who eat wheat are more/less/equal.

❖ Compared to those who eat wheat, children eating *ragi* are more/less.

Preparing for the Class Drama

All children of a class are getting ready for a drama. Some children are acting. Some are busy collecting the dresses. Some are bringing tables and chairs to make the sets.

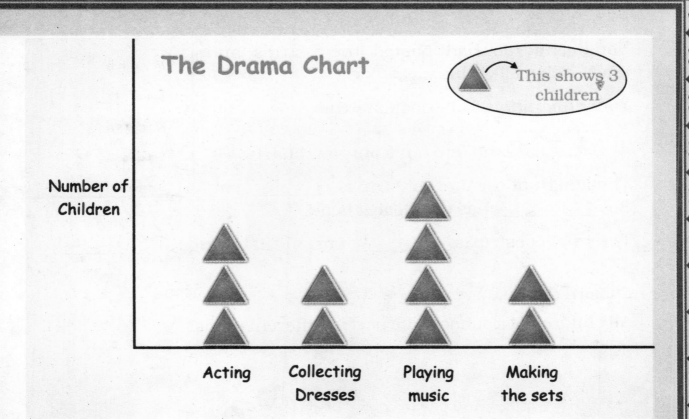

The Drama Chart

This shows 3 children

Number of Children

Acting | Collecting Dresses | Playing music | Making the sets

a) How many children are acting in the drama?

b) Which are more — children making the sets or those acting?

c) What is being done by most of the children?

d) How many children are collecting dresses?

Whose Head is Bigger?

Cut long paper strips from waste paper.

Give one strip to each of your friends. Now put the paper strip around your head and tear off the extra strip. On a big sheet, paste these paper strips along a line.

Some children had pasted their strips and made a chart like this.

Your chart should also look like this.

| Madhu |
| Rohit |
| Ramesh |
| Sadiq |
| Sameena |

❖ Use a scale and find out from your chart:

The length of the longest strip is _____ cm. So _____ has the biggest head.

The smallest strip is _____ cm long. It belongs to _____.

Chapati Chart

All children of a school take part in different clubs:

The *Chapati* Chart shows the number of children in different clubs.

Games Clubs

Garden Club

Drawing Club

From the picture we can see that:

a)   Half the children in the class take part in the Games Club.

b)   One fourth of the children are members of the Garden Club.

c)   The Drawing Club has one fourth of the children of the class.

If there are 200 students in the school, look at the above *Chapati* Chart and tell the number of members in each club:

❖ The Games Club has _____ members.

❖ The Garden Club has _____ members.

❖ There are _____ members in the Drawing Club.

Getting Wet in the Rain

Who likes to get wet in the rain? A child made this *Chapati* Chart after asking his friends.

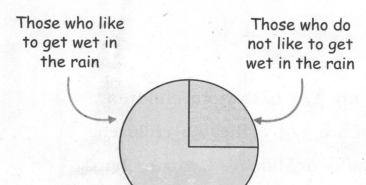

See the *Chapati* Chart and tell:

1) How many children like to get wet in the rain?

    a) half   b) one-fourth   c) three-fourth

2) How many children do not like to get wet in the rain?

    a) half   b) one-fourth   c) three-fourth

If the number of children in the class is 28, then tell the number of children

❖ who like to get wet in the rain _____

❖ who do not like to get wet in the rain _____

Tea, Coffee or Milk

Some children were asked which of these they liked most — Tea, Coffee or Milk.

The drink they like	Number of children
Milk	20
Coffee	10
Tea	10
Total Number of children	_____

Find out from the table:

❖ Children who like milk are $\frac{1}{2}$ / $\frac{1}{4}$ of the total children.

❖ Children who like coffee are $\frac{1}{2}$ / $\frac{1}{4}$ of the total children.

Show the liking for Tea, Coffee or Milk in a *Chapati* Chart.

Kritika Dhoot, Class IX, Ujjain, MP

Anu Damor, Class III, Indore, MP

Farida Husain, Class VI, Faizabad, UP

425

राष्ट्रीय शैक्षिक अनुसंधान और प्रशिक्षण परिषद्
NATIONAL COUNCIL OF EDUCATIONAL RESEARCH AND TRAINING

ISBN 81-7450-698-5

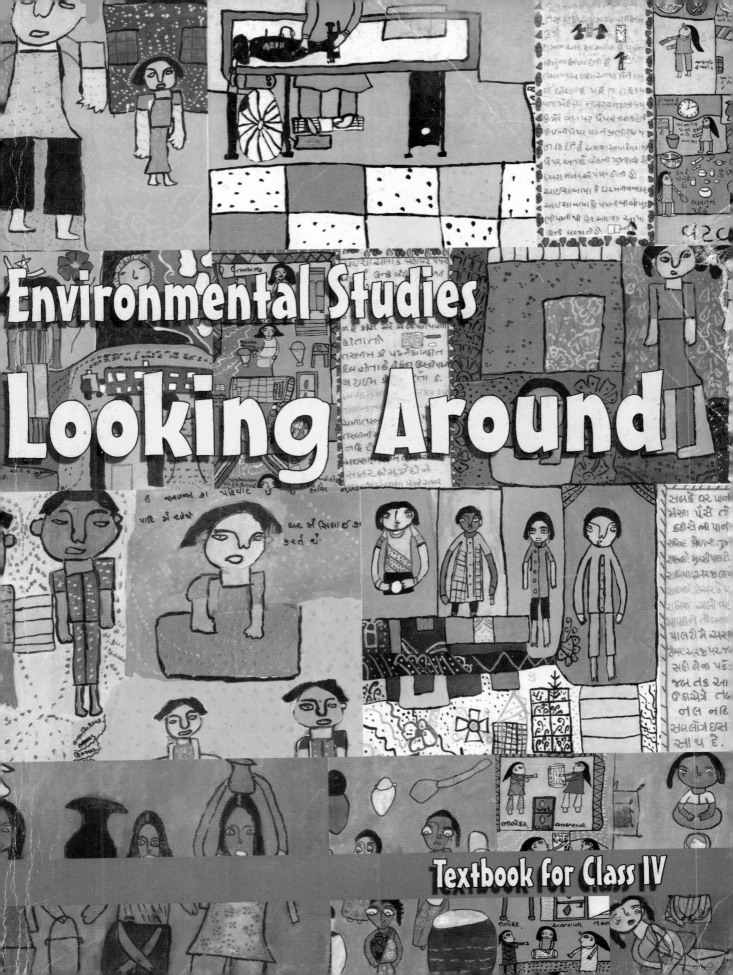

Environmental Studies
Looking Around

Textbook for Class IV